W9-BLK-258

My Dear Ross,
For your love
of baseball — may
it only keep growing
Happy Hanukah
2003
Mom and Dad

GLOVE AFFAIRS

The Romance, History, and Tradition of the Baseball Glove

NOAH LIBERMAN

TRIUMPH
B O O K S
CHICAGO

Copyright © 2003 by Noah Liberman

No part of this publication may be reproduced, stored in a
retrieval system, or transmitted, in any form by any means,
electronic, mechanical, photocopying, or otherwise, without
the prior written permission of the publisher, Triumph Books,
601 S. LaSalle St., Suite 500, Chicago, Illinois 60605.

Library of Congress Cataloging-in-Publication Data

Liberman, Noah, 1961–
   Glove affairs: the romance, history, and tradition of the baseball glove / Noah Liberman.
      p. cm.
   Includes index.
   ISBN 1-57243-420-1 (hc)
   1. Baseball gloves—United States. I. Title: Romance, history, and tradition of the baseball
   glove. II. Title.

   GV879.7 .L53 2003
   796.357'028—dc21

                                        2002073258

This book is available in quantity at special discounts for
your group or organization. For further information, contact:

Triumph Books
601 South LaSalle Street
Suite 500
Chicago, Illinois 60605
(312) 939-3330
Fax (312) 663-3557

Printed in China
ISBN 1-57243-420-1
Interior design by Carney Design, Inc.

To the memory of Myron Liberman and Paul Cardwell,
who loved their families and baseball besides.

CONTENTS

Foreword

———

Growing up in our neighborhood on The Hill in St. Louis, we'd play every game you could think of: baseball, soccer, football, corkball, roller hockey, softball, Indian rubber. Nobody had much of anything in those days, so we'd scrape up any equipment we could find. Baseball gloves, especially new ones, were a rarity.

When I was about 11 or 12, my pop, who was from the Old World and didn't understand American sports, asked me what I wanted for Christmas. I told him I'd like a soccer ball, sneakers, and a baseball glove. And he said, "Well, which one?"

Since baseball was my favorite thing, I wanted a glove. I got a pair of trousers instead. Like I said, Pop thought games were a waste of time. Eventually I got my own glove, a fielder's mitt, when I played American Legion ball. I cherished it and liked working it in. I liked the feel of worn leather. Mostly I loved the fact that the glove was mine. I don't think it matters how old you are, or the level of ball you play—there's nothing more personal than your own baseball glove.

When I became a catcher with the Yankees in the late forties, the mitts were pillow-like, thick and bulky. You'd hear the ball go thunk, but flexibility, especially on foul tips or foul pops, wasn't too good. So I tried one Rawlings with fishnet webbing. And since I loved a well-worn glove, I used that same one for years. I worked it in so much that a few of our pitchers started complaining that their pitches weren't making enough sound. I'd just tell them to stop moaning and throw harder.

Being a catcher, where you squat for three hours and get bruises, bumps, and even broken fingers, you better use your equipment good. Especially your glove. I guess I was tired of getting my fingers numbed—guys like Allie Reynolds and Vic Raschi could throw pretty darn hard—so I started looping my index finger on the outside. People say I'm the first to do that; I don't know. All I know is it helped.

In all my years of playing baseball, I didn't save much. Why keep a uniform? Or an old bat? There was no such thing as a memorabilia business then. But one thing I did keep, and it brings back good memories, is the glove I used to catch Don Larsen's perfect game in the 1956 World Series. Our clubhouse guy, Pete Sheehy, had it bronzed after the game, and I've always kept it. It's now encased in our museum and learning center, on the campus of Montclair State University.

Not long after our museum opened in 1998, the first exhibit was on the history of the baseball glove. I'll tell you, people really enjoyed it. It was well designed by John Golomb, who repairs and custom makes baseball gloves, and whose grandfather started the Everlast sporting goods company. I think kids were amazed seeing those small, prehistoric gloves they used in the 19th century, especially compared to today's craftsmanship.

The nice thing about baseball gloves is that it threads history. Technology has changed, but the gloves are still leather, and still protect you. And because good defense is so important, good gloves are important.

As I said, I was pretty attached to my catcher's glove. I felt it gave me an edge. I always thought Jorge Posada might like to catch with that style of webbing, so a couple of years ago I asked him to try it. After Golomb stitched in my old style webbing in one of Posada's mitts, Posada felt strange. He didn't take to it and felt awkward telling me that. But I understood. It was nothing personal—it's just that a baseball glove *is* personal.

—Yogi Berra

Acknowledgments

When I started my research, I assumed I was the only person with a curious interest in baseball gloves. I was wrong. This book benefits from the enthusiasm of a legion of glove lovers headed by Joe Phillips, publisher of *The Glove Collector* newsletter, who graciously answered hundreds of e-mails from a rank novice trying to learn. Joe loves baseball gloves, and this love informs his newsletter, which in turn informs everyone else. Facts, anecdotes, and attitudes first published in *The Glove Collector* form the backbone of this book, and my debt to Joe can't be repaid. Denny Esken, who some say knows more about Rawlings gloves than Rawlings Sporting Goods itself does, answered questions in his unique way and graciously provided the gorgeous and valuable glove that adorns this book's cover, a Mickey Mantle "gamer" now on display at the National Baseball Hall of Fame. The Hall was kind enough to pull the glove from its display and photograph it expertly. Rawlings had the courage to lend me many valuable old catalogues, whose splendid glove art fills many pages of this book. And many Rawlings executives, especially Chuck Malloy, were more than generous with their time. Mike Seawel of Glovesmith Inc. gave me a fascinating introduction to the art of fine glovemaking. Wilson Sporting Goods and its executives made kind contributions. MastroNet Inc. provided fine photos of gloves from its auctions, and one of its authenticators, Dave Bushing, had all sorts of interesting stories to tell about gloves and about himself. Glove experts helped at every turn, Dick Stump, John Golomb, Gordon Eaton, Mike Tinney, and Chuck Lutomski among them. Wise students of baseball Mark Simon, Steve Steinberg, Tony Craine, Anne Zacharias-Walsh, and John Walsh were helpful in many ways. A glove is nothing without an owner, and scores of additional glove owners are heard in the pages of this book.

A book is perforce a family effort, and my dear wife, Jennifer, was encouraging and patient for every day of the two years I spent on this one. Then she designed it, from cover to lovely cover. My mother, Mathilda Liberman, was the book's first and best reader, and she contributed in countless other ways. My love goes out to my family, as does my sincere gratitude to them and everyone else mentioned here.

A kind uncle bought future Chicago White Sox owner Jerry Reinsdorf his first glove;
his mother put him up to this pose in a ballfield in his hometown of Brooklyn, New York.

Courtesy of Jerry Reinsdorf.

CHAPTER 1

A Kid's Best Friend:
Remembering Your First Glove

"August 11, 1955, my favorite birthday present, now I can play with my brothers."

—*an anonymous handwritten note, folded and stored inside a small, white,
Cosmo-brand kid's glove, where glove collector Ron Carlson found it 45 years later*

Do you remember your first glove? Or the one that meant the most to you? Almost everyone does. A few people don't. More on that later.

Jerry Reinsdorf, owner of the Chicago White Sox and the Chicago Bulls, has a photo in his Comiskey Park office of himself at the age of nine or ten, pitching a baseball in a Brooklyn park. He remembers the nice clothes and the shoes he had on: "They were street shoes, not ball shoes," he says. He remembers the circumstances. "It was a posed picture. I wasn't really playing. My mother must have made me pose for that one." But he remembers the glove more than anything.

"I was about nine, and my parents couldn't afford to buy me the one I'd wanted for a long, long time. So an uncle, Al Improta, gave it to me for my birthday. It was a big thrill, the nicest thing I'd had at that time in my life, my most expensive material possession.

"And I remember my uncle and his brother played catch with me the day they gave me the glove."

Kirby Puckett was no older than seven or eight when his father bought him the state-of-the-art Wilson A2000. He was still using A2000s when he retired more than 30 years later. Courtesy of Wilson Sporting Goods.

The gangly boy in the photo foreshadows today's Reinsdorf. He mixes sports with business, aggressively but sometimes not gracefully. He's sentimental about the glove but pragmatic about the material possession.

His contradictions don't play well with fans, but give him credit for this: he remembers his first glove. Do you?

Maybe you remember who helped you get it.

Kirby Puckett saw a newspaper ad in the late sixties for the A2000, Wilson's top model. "We weren't on welfare or nothing, but right on the edge, and my dad told us never steal anything, just ask." So Puckett asked, and at lunch the next day his father went to Sportmart and bought him one. "As a kid, if you had a Wilson A2000 you had it going on, you know?" Puckett says. He was just six or seven at the time, and he used only A2000s for the next 31 years. He retired with six Gold Gloves.

Omar Vizquel tells of giving an instructional league acquaintance a glove after the man spoke of his two young sons in Colombia, ready to start baseball. "Three years ago I met this guy named Jolbert Cabrera on the team and he told me the story about his dad giving him a glove I gave him 12 years ago. It's a really cool story, and I tell it to everyone because the world is so small."

NBA commissioner David Stern remembers that his dad helped him buy his first glove, but things get hazy after that. He thinks it was a Wilson but admits it might have been a Rawlings. A New York Giants fan, he thinks it might have been a Don Mueller model. "If not, try Stan Musial, even though he was a lefty," Stern says.

Greg Maddux's was already in the family—"my dad's old SSK, and I'm out there at shortstop, eight or nine years old, and the glove was huge, bigger than me," he says. Today the perennial Gold Glover uses the biggest glove of any pitcher in the game.

Kenny Lofton's first glove wasn't too big, but it was still wrong. "I won it at a carnival or something," he told a magazine. "I'm left-handed but it was a right-handed glove. I played with that glove for a whole summer. It worked for me, so I didn't mind." Dave Winfield's first glove was for the correct hand, but the little boy put it on the wrong hand the first time. As an adult, he won seven Gold Gloves.

Sometimes a first glove isn't even a baseball glove. Larry Walker's first was his hockey goaltender mitt, worn to the sandlot. Sammy Sosa and Tony Fernandez have talked about using empty cardboard milk cartons, cutting a hole in the bottom and slits for their fingers midway up.

The stories of those Dominican stars point up how the memory of your first or favorite glove can be tied to your financial circumstances. Bill Mazeroski dug an outhouse for his uncle to earn the money for his first glove, a three-fingered Rawlings Playmaker that was the rage among young players after the war. Cuban defector Rene Arocha, who pitched in the majors for four years in the nineties, said his first glove was pulled from a garbage can, and he could remember how his fingers protruded from holes in the palm. And Seiji Ozawa, the longtime musical director of the Boston Symphony Orchestra, has recalled how his mother sewed him a glove out of scrap canvas and other materials in the tough times in Japan shortly after World War II.

There's a good chance you remember the player whose autograph sat in the palm of your first glove. In CNN host Larry King's favorite, it was Billy Cox's, the slickest-fielding third baseman before

Playmakers

Exclusive Playmaker Design
Assures "Feel of the Fingers"
• • • • • • • • • • •

PM 16

PM16—Playmaker Model Fielders Glove. A full size Playmaker with quality features. Good grade glove leather with full welted seams and full leather lined. Leather bound edges. Solid leather tied-down ball trap with adjustable laced fingers. Patented palm crotch extension (Pat. No. 2,311,949). Shaped hinged pad. Hand oil treated. **List each $9.95**
Trade each $7.45

PM 20

PM20—Playmaker Model Fielders Glove. Made on new, fuller professional pattern with slightly shorter fingers. Tan color glove leather. Full leather lined. Shaped, hinged pad, all seams leather welted, bound edges, laced heel. Leather laced fingers. New solid tied-down ball trap. A fine glove for younger players. Hand oil treated.
List each $7.45

PM 28

PM28—Playmaker Model Fielders Glove. Youth's size Playmaker glove. Playmaker design with hinged pad and Deep Well pocket. Leather laced fingers and new solid leather ball trap. Full palm and finger lining. Laced heel. All seams leather welted. Hand oil treated. Palm crotch extension (Pat. No. 2,311,949).
List each $4.95

PM 32

PM32—Playmaker Model Fielders Glove. New youth's size Playmaker glove. Playmaker design with hinged pad and Deep Well pocket. Patented palm crotch extension (Pat. No. 2,311,949). Full palm and finger leather lined. Adjustable finger lace. Solid leather ball trap. Closed heel. Bound edges, hand oil treated.
List each $3.75

PM 35

PM35—Playmaker Model Fielders Glove. Enlarged Small Size Playmaker. Bound edges. Palm leather lined. Inner greased pocket. Adjustable ball trap. Hinged pad. Laced fingers. Not oiled.
List each $2.45

Page 7

Worth it: Bill Mazeroski dug an outhouse for his uncle to earn the money for his first glove, a Rawlings Playmaker like one of these. Courtesy of Rawlings Sporting Goods.

Brooks Robinson—the slickest ever, according to Casey Stengel.

"My idol was Cox, and when the Dodgers got him in '48 I was 14 years old, and I just took to him," King says. "He had a habit of holding his glove in his right hand when the pitcher was winding up, and he'd slip it onto his left as the pitcher delivered. On the playground, I tried to do it the same way as Billy Cox."

King saved his grocery-delivery money and bought a Cox model at a Davega sporting goods store in Brooklyn. "I shoe-polished it. It had to have a black pocket because it looked right, and we had a theory the ball stayed in the pocket if it had the polished black look."

Hall of Fame pitcher Jim Palmer spent his first 10 years in New York City, and he had the same approach to picking a glove. "If you grew up a Yankee fan and Mickey Mantle was your favorite player, when you went to a sports shop you bought a Mantle glove," he says.

Well, usually. Actor Joe Mantegna has a different take. He and his work, such as the play *Bleacher Bums*, make it clear he's a Cubs fan. But his first glove, a gift "from my dad or somebody," was a Billy Pierce, with the signature of the White Sox' fine left-hander. "All during those years I can remember the Cubs vs. Sox rivalry, but I don't think it ever crossed my mind or made a difference that I was using a Billy Pierce glove. Maybe it even gave me some kind of sympathy or compassion for him. It's kind of interesting."

Michael Perlin, a law school professor in New York City, isn't quite so philosophical. "I grew up in Perth Amboy [New Jersey], and there were two sporting goods stores in that town then," he told *The Times*, a Trenton, New Jersey, newspaper, a few years ago. "My dad was good friends with one of the owners and of course it was at that store where I bought my glove. Trouble was, the only glove he had that fit me was a Ted Lepcio glove, and I had my heart set on a Johnny Temple glove."

Television personality Keith Olbermann had a lot of public fun pointing out the errors in Ken Burns' 1994 *Baseball* miniseries. And he takes even his own parents to task over the provenance of his first glove. "My first glove was a Don Larsen model, which I think they gave me for my ninth birthday. Where on earth they found a new Don Larsen glove in 1968 I'll never know." It's a good point. Larsen didn't have an endorsed glove after 1959 or

1960, so it looks like Olbermann's folks bought him an eight-year-old glove.

If it's not the endorsement on your first glove, it might be the smell that makes you nostalgic. Bill Bradley, NBA Hall of Famer and former senator, remembers a Marty Marion Rawlings first baseman's glove his parents gave him in his home town, Crystal City, Missouri. "I always remember going to the glove store for weeks and smelling the leather, wondering how long the smell would remain so strong."

Randy Hundley, who won a Gold Glove with the Cubs, also spent a lot of time at the store. "When I decided I wanted to catch I was, shucks, seven or eight, and I went to a sporting goods store and found this mitt that just fit my hand perfectly.

This was back in 1950 or so, but the bloomin' thing was $75.

"So I used to walk home every day and go by the store to make sure they hadn't sold the thing, and after a month the owner called my dad and said, 'Randy's in here every day looking at that mitt, and he holds it and smells it and puts it on his hand and looks at it. I know it's expensive but I'll try to make you a deal.'" Hundley got the glove. He figures it was about 50 dollars.

Now, do you remember what happened to that glove that meant so much? New York Yankees star center fielder Bernie Williams says his first "formal" glove was a tan Sears Ted Williams model, and he wore it from the age of 13 until his first pro game, in winter league during his junior year in

"The Fragrance Organ, also on the first floor, is a circular scent bar that at first looks like a made-to-order perfumerie, with 490 bottles of oils. It's designed to be both educational and fun. A gloved individual dips a paper wand into the bottle of your choice and passes it under your nose for a sniff. You can smell just about any aroma, from gardenias to bubble gum to the scent of a new baseball glove. After you've had your fill, a bowl of coffee beans is offered to cleanse the airways."

—From the *San Francisco Chronicle,* December 8, 1998

BASEBALL FIELDERS GLOVES

MARTY MARION

G600—Marty Marion Fielders Glove. Designed in collaboration with Marty Marion, famous major leaguer. A medium sized professional "Deep Well" model. Made of selected Tan color glove leather. Pro-Laced "U" crotch. Streamlined type fingers and thumb, shaped hand-formed pad and floating heel. Adjustable laced fingers. Pocket is Inner-Greased and has great depth. Entire glove leather lined. All seams leather welted, roll leather bound edges. Closed heel. Broad wrist strap. Adjustable solid ball trap. An excellent, light, flexible glove.

Trade each $9.25   List each $12.25

Doug Rader's Little League glove meant so much to him that he used it all the way into the major leagues. It was a Rawlings Marty Marion, like this one.

Courtesy of Rawlings Sporting Goods.

high school. Ivan Calderon spotted it and demanded, "Dude, what are you doing playing with that glove?" He gave the kid a pro-level Rawlings. Says Williams, "A week later I ask him, 'So how much do I owe you?' and he said, 'Are you kidding, man?'" Williams still uses Rawlings gloves.

Doug Rader, who won five straight Gold Gloves at third base with the Houston Astros, wore the same glove from the sandlot to the pros too. "My dad scrimped and saved and bought me a Marty Marion Rawlings in Little League. It had the button on the back at the wrist, the old-style glove. I used it until my second full year in the majors when it rotted off my hand. This was 1968 and I was 23."

A few years later, future Twins and Cubs executive Andy MacPhail had a similar experience. In the early seventies at Dickinson College he was a strong-armed right fielder—"allegedly," he says. "I mean,

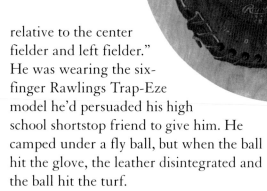

"When you got a finger-hole glove when you were a kid, that was, like, the coolest glove." Veteran catcher Eddie Taubensee is talking about Rawlings' Fastback design with the Holdster slot. When former big-league catcher and manager Joel Skinner was a kid in the seventies, *"red gloves were the craze,"* he *says.* Courtesy of Rawlings Sporting Goods.

XFCB17-5

relative to the center fielder and left fielder." He was wearing the six-finger Rawlings Trap-Eze model he'd persuaded his high school shortstop friend to give him. He camped under a fly ball, but when the ball hit the glove, the leather disintegrated and the ball hit the turf.

"I was jogging to the dugout after the inning and my coach demanded the glove. He turned it inside out and told me it was a piece of garbage and punted it over the fence. That might be an emblem for my baseball career."

If you were lucky, you got the glove everyone wanted. "When I was a kid, red gloves were the craze. Everyone in the big leagues was using one," says Joel Skinner,

who caught for nine major league seasons. His dad, then a Padres coach, got him a red Rawlings Larry Bowa with a basket web after Pete Rose gave his brother a red MacGregor.

Veteran Cleveland Indians infielder Travis Fryman recalls that his Rawlings was "similar to what Cal Ripken used or Alex Rodriguez uses today, with the T-web and the finger hole in back." Fryman's former teammate Eddie Taubensee says, "When you got a finger-hole glove when you were a kid, that was, like, the coolest glove." They mean the Fastback design with the Holdster slot, patented by Rawlings in 1971 and found exclusively on their gloves for the 17 years of the patent's life.

Whatever happened to that old glove? Skinner's fell off his bike rack on the way to practice. "I must have retraced my tracks for a week and never found my glove, and it killed me, just killed me," he says.

ESPN host Dan Patrick had a big Willie Mays MacGregor that he used at shortstop. "I used it for 15 years until some guy stole it out of my trunk in college. It was so frayed and torn and patched with another piece of leather, I can't imagine what anyone else would have wanted with that glove," he says.

And pugnacious sportswriter/TV commentator Peter Vecsey has an "almost" lost-glove story that could only have happened to him. "I was a big Brooklyn Dodger fan, and I'd always come over from Queens with my friend and we'd always get lost. But I loved Duke Snider, and we'd sit in the center-field bleachers. One day my friend just throws my glove on the field, and I'm frantic. I yelled to Snider to throw it back— and he gives me the finger! I was stunned, tears streaming down my face. So in between innings, Carl Furillo comes over and gets the glove and tosses it back to me." Did Furillo become Vecsey's favorite then? "You better believe it."

Successful longtime NBA coach and executive Frank Layden, a former Niagara University first baseman, has another offbeat story, this one about a sort-of first glove. "I love baseball more than basketball. And I love the theater most of all," he begins. (This would please Mantegna.) Anyway, Layden goes to three dozen Salt Lake Stingers minor league games a year, sits behind the visitors' dugout, and sings "Take Me Out to the Ballgame" on top of that same dugout.

And he wears a glove during the game. He bought it a while ago at a Fred Meyer retail store for about $25. "I'm buying the glove and the lady says, 'Hi Mr. Layden, how nice, you're getting this for your grandson?' and I said 'Hell no! I'm getting it for me!'"

It's fun to remember that first glove. It's sentimental and it might be a bit bittersweet. So you can only imagine what two of the greatest glove men in history have to say about their first. What piece of leather did Brooks Robinson first slip on his hand in Little Rock 60 years ago? What glove did Ozzie Smith wear when the Wizard was just an apprentice?

"I don't remember," both say.

From the first attested use in 1870 to the last barehanded holdout in 1896,
nearly three decades passed before gloves were universal in the major leagues.
Suffering was one of the game's manly traditions. From the Rucker Archive.

CHAPTER 2

Born in Shame: The First Gloves

*"Fred Pfeffer is playing second base without gloves.
He lost his glove in Philadelphia and was rather glad to be rid of it, as he considers
gloves more of a hindrance than a help to infielders."*

—from Sporting Life *of June 17, 1893*

The baseball glove began its life in shame.

In the early days of professional baseball, a defensive wizard wasn't a *gloveman*, because real men didn't wear gloves. No one did. Pro ball in the last third of the 19th century was a he-man affair, and part of the deal was you put up with the pain and disfigurement from catching that small, hard ball. But when you'd caught eight games in nine days, as Doug Allison had, and you'd injured your left hand several times already that season handling the "swift" pitches (as they were described) of Cincinnati Red Stockings pitchers, you put comfort over valor.

The *Cincinnati Commercial* reported on June 28, 1870: "Allison caught to-day in a pair of buckskin mittens, to protect his hands." This dry note was tucked into a story on the team's game against the Washington Nationals, and it buried the news, as a reporter would say. For the first time on record, a major leaguer had worn a glove in a game. He was razzed by opposing players and fans. No mention is found of any other player wearing a glove for another five years.

When Allison donned his mittens, baseball was already America's game. It had firm rules and paid professionals, and some of its traditions stretched back at least a century. Historians peg the beginning of "modern" baseball to 1845, when Alexander Cartwright and the amateur New York Knickerbocker Base Ball Club issued a set of rules much like today's. Actually, the word *base-ball* was first used back in 1762. But historians show a funny aversion to considering those earlier diamond games baseball. They're put off by rules that allowed the defense to "plug" or "soak" a runner with a thrown ball for an out or that allowed players to run clockwise. Baseball's bible, *Total Baseball*, begins its "Famous Firsts" section with Cartwright's rule book in 1845, ignoring the more vital firsts (such as balls, strikes, and bases) that came well before and implying that a clerical event marked the beginning of the game we now play. That's an arbitrary way to make sense of a long evolution.

Whatever their take on modern baseball, in more expansive moods, those same historians say ballgames began in Egypt three millennia ago. Then they trace an evolution through Middle Eastern fertility rites and European churchyard festivals, right down to Allison's Red Stockings, the first professional baseball team.

The historical questions are diverting, but this is for certain: all those games had balls to catch. By the 1300s, they had bases to run to. But never, until Allison, is there firm evidence that they had gloves.

Although the papers are silent on gloves in the major leagues after Allison's transgression, sporting goods catalogs began offering them to the public as early as 1872, and the authoritative annual *DeWitt's Guide* of 1872 reads: "The catcher will find it advantageous when facing swift pitching to wear tough leather gloves, with the fingers cut off near the joint, as they will prevent him having his hands split and puffed up."

But bare-handedness was so ingrained in the ethos of the game that when an exception was made for catchers, like Allison, it was made for no one else for five years. Charlie Waitt was a soft-hitting outfielder for the St. Louis Brown Stockings in 1875, his first of four journeyman seasons. That year he played a few games at first base. Evidently he discovered that dead-ball-era pegs from a shortstop stung a lot more than dead-ball-era pop flies. So one day he sidled out to the bag with a thin, half-fingered, unpadded glove on. It was

Cincinnati catcher Doug Allison (left) might have been the first pro to wear a glove, in 1870. Albert Spalding (right) said it was Charlie Waitt in 1875— but Spalding might have had an ulterior motive.
From the Rucker Archive.

flesh-colored, because he hoped no one would notice. But everyone did, and he caught hell.

No first baseman wore a glove for another two years because of the stigma. Finally Chicago great Albert Spalding, who was moving to first base from pitcher in 1877, made gloves for first basemen stick when he slipped on a pair of black ones and, he later wrote, evoked sympathy rather than hilarity. Like Waitt, he was moving to first from another position with fewer hard shots

to field—in fact, outfielders and pitchers were the last to convert to gloves, several years later. But Spalding also had fame on his side and the profit motive: soon he was scheming to sell those very gloves in his sporting goods store for between $1 and $2.50. *

(Not coincidentally, the catcher's mask was first used in a pro game in 1877 as well. It had been invented in 1873, and its first known use in organized ball was by Harvard student James Tyng in 1875, the very same year as Waitt's short experiment.)

Events have a way of obscuring the past, and so it is with Spalding's glove milestone. Despite him and the success of the sporting goods company that still bears his name, the official glove of Major League Baseball is the Wilson—it's never been a Spalding. The semiofficial Gold Glove award was Rawlings' idea in 1957, not Spalding's. In fact, Rawlings even owned Spalding for a short time in the late fifties and made gloves for Spalding in the sixties. Spalding was the game's official ball for a long while, that is until Rawlings took over

* The chronology detailed here is the surest given the available evidence. There's correspondence that suggests gloves were used in the Massachusetts Game decades earlier, but this was an all-amateur form of baseball, in which some experimentation might not be surprising.

The "Pointers" section of a 1929 Shapleigh's sporting goods catalog says gloves were invented in 1867, when a sore-handed third baseman for the Rockford, Illinois, team put on a special glove with an "armored" palm. It doesn't give names. The trouble with this account is that the pitcher for that very team was Albert Spalding himself, then 16 years old. One would hope that he would have remembered this and mentioned the sore-handed third baseman in his 1911 memoir, where he tells us of Waitt—although Spalding might not have been above stretching the truth if it suited him.

In fact, Spalding's account of the birth of the glove raises more questions than this one. In his memoir he writes that Waitt wore "the first glove I ever saw on the hand of a ballplayer." He not only does not mention the Rockford player, he never mentions Allison either, although Allison played on opposing teams during Spalding's entire eight-year pro career. If Allison's gloves had caught on, would Spalding have claimed Waitt was the first? And even if Allison wore his gloves only once, isn't it likely that Spalding, who became a sporting-goods entrepreneur, would have had an ear for the story? It's possible that baseball had so thoroughly accepted the catcher's mitt in 1875 that Spalding could call Waitt's "the first" and mean it—that the novelty now was a fielder wearing a glove. Or perhaps Spalding had a very bad or very selective memory. In fact, what if Spalding purposely forgot Allison—and maybe even his Rockford teammate—for the sake of his own reputation? Corporate chiefs have been known to lie, of course.

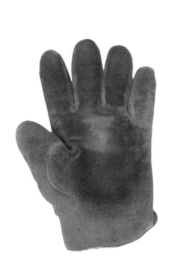

An 1890s fielder's glove, now called a "workman's" glove by collectors. Sold in a Mastronet auction. Copyright © MastroNet Inc.

in 1977. So Spalding's association with the game now is only historical and evolutionary. It does make the official ball of the National Basketball Association, but if you're a baseball fan, do you really care?

So if we believe him, Spalding cleared the way, and major leaguers at all positions began to accept the idea of saving their manly but sore hands. Most infielders had jumped on board in a few years, and outfielders and pitchers joined them several years later. To picture the gloves they wore, think of today's driving gloves—thin leather, open back, half fingers—one on each hand. Two-handed was always the way

to catch baseballs, and gloves weren't nearly big or soft enough yet to encourage one-handed grabs. But the slow evolution had begun.

In 1882, Providence shortstop Arthur Irwin broke two fingers on one hand and approached the Draper-Maynard Sporting Goods company with the idea of padding sewn right into his glove. It had to work better than the wads of grass and slabs of meat catchers were using then. It was easily enough done, using an oversized, half-fingered buckskin driving glove. And when John Montgomery Ward, a top player of the day, adopted the new glove, it took off. Players began wearing a padded half-finger

Starting in 1884, pitchers could throw overhand— although they still stood a tight 50 feet from the plate. By 1888 the mitt had been invented and patented. This tintype was done in the mid-1890s; the catcher's mask was already almost two decades old by then.

From the Rucker Archive.

glove on their nonthrowing hand and an unpadded half-glove on the other hand. On the nonthrowing hand, imagine a Wells-Lamont workman's glove with padded palm. The back was open, with a buttoned strap or rawhide lacing to cinch it tight. By 1884, nearly every player was wearing one, except for pitchers and some outfielders. By 1886 most players had gone to a single padded glove, on their catching hand, with full fingers.

A few players still weren't satisfied, and they innovated. Catchers had the most at stake: in 1884, the rules were changed and pitchers could throw overhand, from the then-standard distance of 50 feet—10 feet, six inches closer than today's! Joe Gunson of the Kansas City Blues had the fingers of his glove sewn together in 1888; then he added sheep's wool padding around them, secured it with wire, and covered the whole mess with a buckskin mitt.* Two decades after Allison, baseball still frowned on letting hands get comfortable, and Gunson was razzed. Probably the other team said something about him wearing an oven mitt. But

this time it didn't take two years for a good idea to catch on. It took just a few weeks, and soon every catcher had one. A year later the idea was patented.

The inspiration for Gunson's idea might have been Detroit's Jim "Deacon" White, a third baseman who had recently sewn a "leather plate on the face of his infielder's glove and thereby got good results with liners," according to one source. And Gunson's mitt made sense to more than just catchers. For nearly two decades, starting in the 1890s, there were fielder's *mitts*. They look quaint to our eyes, and they were never as popular as gloves, which made players just a bit more dexterous.

We're now a dozen years down the road from Albert Spalding's calculated risk in 1877, but for proof of the strength of tradition, understand that no pitcher wore a glove for yet another four years, until Cleveland's George Cuppy in 1893. Imagine what the game was like back then. One early commentator wrote that shaking a catcher's hand in the days before Gunson was like "grasping a handful of peanuts."

---

* Another account has Gunson's glove without the wire but a Ted Kennedy adding the wire and patenting it. At least the date, 1888, isn't in dispute.

No. B1—Rawlings... is superior to any on the market... in a manner that will insure durability and satisfaction... requirements of a Baseman's Mitt, and conforms nicely to the hand. The ... heel are extra well padded. Guaranteed superior to any similar Mitt on the market.
Each $3 00

No. A2—Rawlings Professional First Baseman's Mitt. This Mitt is made in the manner and general finish as our No. B1 described above, except it is made of selected russet calf skin, which some players prefer to horsehide or buckskin, and is a better Mitt than our competitors furnish at anything near the price .... each, 3 00

No. X5—First Baseman's Mitt. Made of asbestos calf, dark drab color, strong and durable, and warranted not to harden from wetting. Made first-class and the best Mitt of the kind ever offered at the price. This is a bargain .... each 50

Nos. B1-A2-X5.

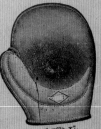

No. X3—First Baseman's and Fielder's Mitt. This Mitt is made of finest quality mouse-colored buckskin, fits closely to the hand, and being very flexible, gives nearly the same freedom of motion as a glove and much better protection to the hand .... each, $2 50

No. X6—First Baseman's and Fielder's Mitt. Made of the finest quality drab buckskin, light padding of best quality hair felt; very soft and pliable. A Mitt that will suit any one .... each, 1 75

No. X6½—First Baseman's and Infielder's Mitt. Made with fine quality horsenide palm, napa green back and fingers; deep ball pockets, well made. A Mitt that will suit.
Each 1 00

No. X7—Boy's First Base Mitt. Made of asbestos calf, gold ooze tan color; strong and durable; made first-class, and warranted not to harden. A Mitt that will please any boy .... each 50

No. X6-X6½-X7.

Fielder's mitts were available 100 years ago, like Rawlings model X6 (above right). Today, the Akadema company markets the same concept (right)—although the small indentations at the finger-tips make this a legal "glove" according to Major League Baseball rules. Courtesy of Rawlings Sporting Goods and Akadema Inc.

Catchers applied tincture of benzoin, a resin from the balsam tree, to toughen their hands. When Chicago catcher "Silver" Flint retired in 1889, he announced that every joint in both fingers had been broken at least once. Irwin, who made padded gloves thinkable, had a pinky that emerged from his hand at a right angle. And Cincinnati scribe Ren Mulford, in the same story in which he coined the term "hot corner" in 1889, wrote that third baseman Hick Carpenter fielded seven line drives and it "almost tore him apart." You'd never read that today. An infielder has little to fear from a line drive as long as his eyes are working.

To avoid injury back then, you went after the ball in a very different way. "We had a trick of making a spring-box of the fingers, the ball seldom hit-ting against the palm, and we could pull down even the hottest liners that way, though broken fingers happened now and then," Cap Anson recalled. And he might have been putting a positive spin on things. Even after the turn of the century, glove-makers' catalogs had to assure players that with their models, you "don't have to ease off the ball." That's no way to turn a double play!

And here's the best story of all. Cincinnati second baseman Bid McPhee held out against gloves. "True, hot-hit balls do sting a little at the opening of the season, but after you get used to it, there is no trouble on that score," he said. Then, for 1896, McPhee gave in. He was already one of the top fielders in the game, but his error total dropped by two-thirds that year. His record .978 fielding average stood for nearly 30 years.

Barehanded 19th century fielders made a "springbox" with their hands and tried to catch the ball in their fingers. From the Rucker Archive.

Almost three decades stood between Allison's desperate little risk and McPhee's final stand, and this tells you what you need to know about the evolution of baseball gloves: it was slow and it was stubborn, from 1875 right on through to 1957, when Wilson brought out the A2000, the first glove—ever—with no flaws.

In the early years, the force of tradition and baseball's manly ethic hampered evolution—in many ways. They encouraged rowdyism and drunkenness, gambling and game-throwing—behavior Spalding sought to change. In a game in the late 1880s, Philadelphia outfielder Ed Andrews thought nothing of running 20 feet inside of third base to score a run while the lone umpire had his back turned. This was bare-knuckles baseball—to literalize a metaphor—so men who wanted to protect their hands with a glove always risked looking sissy. Some players acquiesced in wearing a glove but cut the palm out to prove their toughness. This points to something important about the gloves of the 19th century: they were invented mainly for protection of the fingers, not for protection *and* dazzling catches, like today's gloves.

Still, fielders started turning the tables on hitters. The National Association fielding percentage in 1871, when no one except maybe some catchers wore leather, was .834—eight errors a game—and at least every other run was unearned. The 1885 World Series had 78 errors and 74 runs. By 1900, a few years after McPhee donned his first glove, the National League's average was up to .943. Fielders were now converting an extra chance every nine tries. No doubt some of it had to do with better training, better positioning, and better fields. But Henry Chadwick, the great chronicler of early baseball, wrote before he died in 1908 that gloves were the "father of improved 'inside' baseball." He noted that a player didn't need to have "rugged hands and mighty forearms," so the game was infused with new talent. Infielders became defter and more aggressive because they didn't have to "devote a part of [their] attention and courage to watching out for [their] hands." And catchers could now catch almost anything, making it feasible to allow overhand pitching in 1884. Nine years later, the fly rule was devised because of gloves. Now that catches were more certain, the rule was needed to protect the offense against double plays. All in all, it's impossible to overestimate the effect gloves have had on the game of baseball. Perhaps no innovation has changed the game more.

In 1908, there was one last push in the press against gloves. *Sporting Life* suggested that only catchers be allowed big mitts; pitchers and infielders should wear small gloves and outfielders none at all. The annual *Spalding Guide* (ironically) guessed that there would be no more .400 hitters, as fielders now had "the daring to undertake to stop or catch anything." Imagine that: a fielder no longer had to "ease off." And the *Boston Globe* made an assertion that even today, with team fielding averages around .980, will make your eyes roll: "Men break into the game solely because they can hit. The big mitt does the rest." The *Globe* never saw Bobby Bonilla at third base.

Final proof that gloves would forever be part of the game came in 1910, 35 years after Waitt. Baseball had the Reach Sporting Goods company make a livelier ball and introduced it quietly into the 1910 World Series, a high-scoring affair in which the Philadelphia A's' margin of victory over the Chicago Cubs was better than five runs. The next year, the number of .300 hitters more than doubled, to 57. The glove had secured its place in the game, and in response baseball could do nothing but juice the ball.

Born in shame as protection for hurting hands, the glove had developed slowly, over three decades, into a tool. Over the next six decades, as batters flourished with the lively ball, the glove would be perfected. But even this evolutionary era was slow—odd at first blush, considering the growth of baseball and commerce and manufacturing in the United States. We'll cover this era in the next chapter, questioning why it took 90 years in all to perfect the simple tool that is a leather baseball glove.

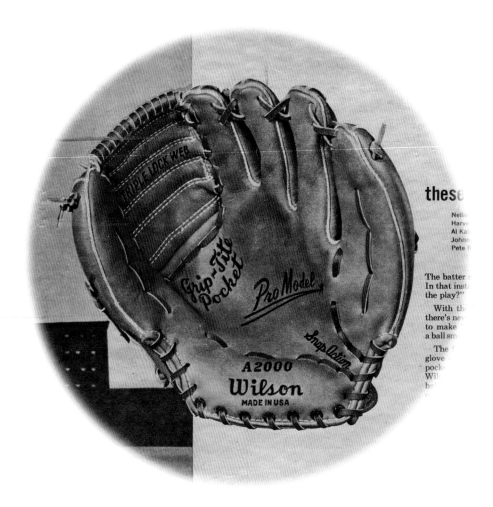

With a bigger web, a better hinge, and a more ergonomic shape, the Wilson A2000 took the baseball world by storm in 1957, stealing the spotlight from longtime leader Rawlings. Courtesy of Wilson Sporting Goods.

Perfection . . . Finally: The Slow Arrival of the Wilson A2000

"I had my picture taken with Home Run Baker. He came to the ballpark in the fifties and I saw the glove he used. I don't know how the hell they caught anything with those gloves, honest to God. The fingers were separated, no lacing there, unbelievable. I said, 'Mr. Baker, how'd you ever catch it with that glove?'"

—*Brooks Robinson*

When Wilbur Wright made the first powered, sustained, and controlled flight in human history in 1903, a baseball glove looked like this:

Courtesy of Rawlings Sporting Goods.

Nos. X00 and X0½.

In 1919, a Curtiss NC-4 became the first plane to cross the Atlantic, and a year later, Rawlings stood the baseball world on its ear, believe it or not, with the introduction of this glove, the Bill Doak model:

first jet plane, went 409 miles per hour. The glove of gloves that year was the Rawlings Red Rolfe "rolled-lace" model, the same kind Al Gionfriddo used in the 1947 World Series to keep a Joe DiMaggio drive from going over the wall in Game 6.

Courtesy of Rawlings Sporting Goods.

Courtesy of Rawlings Sporting Goods.

When Charles Lindbergh made the first solo Atlantic crossing, in 1927, the Doak was still state-of-the-art. The same was true in 1932, when the tiny, stylish Gee Bee R-1 stunt plane hit 252 miles per hour. Are you getting the feeling that baseball gloves evolved very, very slowly?

The Doak was no longer cutting edge (though it was still in the Rawlings catalog) in 1943, when the Bell XP-59-A, America's

Take a look at it and note all the features that appear to make it *hard* to catch the ball. There's the thick, round, stiff thumb and the thick, round, stubby pinkie. There's the heavy padding at the heel. There's no hinge. There's a small pocket, the result of so much padding and no hinge. There are no laces between the fingers. In 1943, 40 years after Wilbur Wright's flight, American pilots were flying jets and

American baseball professionals were still catching balls with pillows. You did your best to catch the ball in the palm then. The rolled-lace web would snare the ball too, but it didn't allow for the quickest return throw. And you didn't get much help from the free-floating fingers if you misplayed a ball against them. This was not optimal design.

Much of this was still very true 10 years later, when the Stan Musial Personal Model was the tops in Rawlings' line:

Courtesy of Rawlings Sporting Goods.

But finally, in 1957, almost 90 years after Doug Allison donned a glove for the first time in a professional game, the Wilson Sporting Goods Company introduced a glove with no significant flaws, the A2000.

The march toward the A2000 was so slow as to be stunning. Why did it take so long? American technology had taken quantum leaps in the previous century and besides, the A2000 didn't require a lot more manufacturing skill than the Bill Doak model had in 1920. Analyze the A2000 itself and you begin to get an answer: The A2000 doesn't

Courtesy of Wilson Sporting Goods.

look like the human hand. It took almost 90 years for ballplayers and glovemakers to shake off the belief—or was it instinct?—that the glove must look like the hand.

The A2000's padding is streamlined, and the fingers, thumb, and heel are flat and thin. How different from a hand, with its fleshy heel and round fingers. The A2000's thumb reaches nearly as high as the fingers do, it's set into the glove at a low point, and it's set quite forward from the palm and web (which was the Doak's masterstroke, in a tentative way). Your hand is not much like this—until you close it around a ball. The A2000 has a fully expressed hinge, the first ever. Your hand has no such thing (it doesn't need it, because the thumb and fingers move brilliantly on their own), but a glove must have one, to allow the hand to do its work.

The A2000 has a large web, larger than any before it. And it has laces connecting the fingers, a feature patented in the twenties but—no surprise here—not widespread until the late forties. And the glove is oriented around an axis that runs diagonally at 40 degrees or so, not due north. Your hand does the same—when you close it. But when you hold your hand wide open, your eye runs straight up through your middle finger; and if you look back through the illustrations in these pages, you see that in

the early days, gloves were oriented this way, too. In most respects, they were like a hand held wide open. The evolution of the glove is, in large part, the slow realization that a glove must reflect how a hand moves to catch a ball, not how it looks when you stare at it.

Fingerlaces exemplify this necessity. Today we can't conceive of a glove without them. The Ken-Wel Company's fine Dazzy Vance model offered fingerlaces in the thirties, but most players rejected the idea because they felt they needed individually articulated fingers to grab the ball—as if they were catching bare-handed. And maybe they did need free fingers, considering how small and shallow the pocket was and how little the glove flexed. But as the glove gradually evolved, as the thumb became more agile and helpful, as the padding was streamlined, a player could trust fingers that were laced together and

Rawlings CEO Stephen O'Hara once told stock analysts that the company had invented "the original split-finger glove, developed by pitcher Bill Doak in 1922." Doak did invent a deeper-pocket glove that quickly became very popular, but "split-finger" is merely our term for gloves with no finger laces—basically every glove until the late forties. Doak did thow a *spit*ball; maybe that's what O'Hara meant.

Not So Fast!

Ken-Wel's fingerlace glove was a good idea whose time hadn't come. Can the same be said for some more recent ideas? Rawlings and Spalding introduced gloves more than 10 years ago that had an inflatable bladder for a secure fit. They picked up on the "pump" technology Reebok was using in its shoes. The Spalding version won a prestigious Industrial Design Excellence Award. One judge, a top Ford Motor executive, called it "the first innovation in baseball gloves in 100 years," apparently unaware of the web, the hinge, and rawhide lacing. Nevertheless, the Spalding glove was discontinued. You'd be lucky to find one in a flea market today. Rawlings' glove was "a bust," a Rawlings executive told

the *Houston Chronicle*. Oh, and five years ago there was Nike's "clamshell" glove idea. It was a firm foam-rubber device with a softer "glove" sewn to the back, where your hand went. It was held together with plastic clips and wire straps. It smelled like plastic. "Baseball gloves have always been brown and leather. Ours will be neither," a Nike executive said. It was part of the company's push to use space-age materials to revolutionize sports equipment. Forget that the company had talked to 200 minor league and college players and, by its own admission, kept hearing, "My glove works fine." It forged ahead. Finally, the effort was discontinued and the glove never was offered for sale.

worked as a unit. The fine shortstop Eddie Joost explains why he took a teammate's advice and rigged up his own fingerlaces in the late thirties. "The Doak [glove], as small as it was, you'd have a ball hit out on the fingers and you would lose it a little bit. Clyde Beck showed me [his laced glove], and the ball just ran into the glove."

In the same way, players gradually began to trust the growing webs. A watershed: catching the ball where your hand wasn't. Joost says the A2000, web and all, was "half again as large as the gloves I had used." And Al Kaline told a reporter: "The A2000 gave you so much confidence, especially when you had to catch the ball with one hand. The glove seemed to automatically collapse around the ball."

The A2000 took the major leagues by storm. Rawlings had dominated the league since the late twenties, and its gloves were on the hands of four of every five major

Ken-Wel's state-of-the-art Dazzy Vance glove was ahead of its time. Players still preferred nonlaced fingers, like the human hand. Fingerlaces became standard after WWII, as gloves began to mimic the hand less and became a superior tool. Note the unusual seams at the bottom of the fingers in back. This Ken-Wel invention prevented tearing under stress. Courtesy of Mike Tinney.

BELLOWS WEB
Newest in web designs. Construction forms "Built-in Trap" web area. Lends itself to errorless performances. (Patent No. 3,590,389)

FASTBACK
Revolutionary Fastback construction. The closed glove concept is designed to provide much greater glove control, a snug, confident fit and split-second flexibility. The end result is a fielding partner that clings to your hand and reacts as you do. The Fastback model (Patent No. 3,576,036) features the Holster finger slot (Patent No. 3,602,915) for even greater glove control. The Fastback is available in fielders gloves, first base mitts and catchers mitts.

BASKET-WEB
Available on fielders gloves, first base mitts and catchers mitts. Most popular web design being offered today — interwoven strips of the finest and softest leather provide the matched strength and flexibility. No break-in period required. (Patent No. 3,321,771)

"DOUBLE CA-THUD" POCKET
Specially constructed toe section with adjustable leather cross-lacing for better glove control in this section. This feature allows the best possible break-in without decreasing the fielding area of the glove. (Patent No. 3,051,958)

DOUBLE LAZY "S" POCKET LACE
Available on fielders gloves and first base mitts. Conforms glove to natural hand position which affords greater flexibility and support. Provides for firm support to the preformed pocket and Hinged Pad.

"HEART-OF-THE-HIDE" LEATHER
The finest leather available for use on gloves and mitts. "Heart-of-the-Hide" leather comes from only the choicest sections of select hides and is then tanned to meet the exact specifications required by Rawlings for the "Professional Player".

EDGE-U-CATED HEEL
A U-shaped heel that is formed by lacing extended up the thumb and little finger providing a sturdy, yet flexible heel area. Adjustable to fit glove to any size hand for greater control and better all around fit. (Patent No. 2,995,757)

FLEX-O-MATIC PALM
Available on fielders gloves and first base mitts. A series of five vertical lacings over a light, flat heel pad providing the wearer with flexibility across the entire width of the heel. Palm design allows for sure-grip throughout entire area of the pocket.

L-HEEL
Available on fielders glove. Leather lacing across the heel and up the little finger producing an L-shaped heel that conforms to the contour of the hand at the wrist area. (Patent No. 2,995,757)

RULE SPECIFICATION
According to professional, collegiate and high school rules, gloves constructed with white leather may not be used by pitchers in official game play.

5

Sentimental trademarks: serious sandlotters recall Rawlings' trademarks, such as the Edge-U-Cated Heel and the Basket Web, with a smile—unless maybe they played Wilson, and instead recall the Grip-Tite-Pocket and Dual Hinge web. Courtesy of Rawlings Sporting Goods.

leaguers in the fifties. Wilson cut into that significantly but never won over a majority of players, because Rawlings quickly countered with similar features—and piled on many more, such as the Edge-U-Cated Heel (a narrow, streamlined heel with lacing running from thumb to pinkie), the Fastback closed-back concept, and the Flex-O-Matic Palm, with its distinctive radial lacing. Mention of these trademarks brings smiles of recognition to the faces of millions of sandlot players, from the fifties to today.

This is the evolution of fielder's gloves specifically, but catchers' mitts and first basemen's mitts have analogous histories. The inset picture on pg. 30 shows an early

RAWLINGS "TRAPPER"

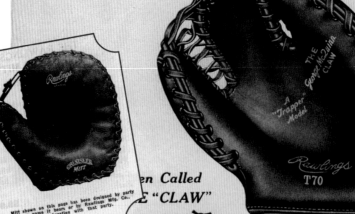

A Rawlings Origination!

NOW PATENTED
(Pat. No. 2,281,315)

THE RAWLINGS "GEORGE SISLER" MITT, the superior of all baseman's mitts, built under the personal supervision and direction of George Sisler, Star first baseman and used by him in all his games. Distinctly a Professional Model, guaranteed to meet the most exacting requirements of professional players.

Built of the finest Willow chrome tanned horse hide, treated with our special Glovolium oil dressing, making the mitt as soft as chamois, yet it stubbornly resists the hardest usage. Panel back, roll leather bound. Inner pad of Asbestos felt, hand formed to make deep natural pocket. Laced with very best chrome tanned lace, Rawlings Patent Buckle Protector at wrist. Neither materials, labor, nor time have been spared to make this mitt the very best that can be made. Made in Rights and Lefts.

Each **$9.90**

—17—

Mitt shown on this page has been designed by party whose name it bears or by Rawlings Mfg. Co., in collaboration with that party.

A twenties base mitt (above) and the innovative Trapper model of two decades later (right).

Courtesy of Rawlings Sporting Goods.

en Called
E "CLAW"

Back View Trapper Mitt

- The sensational mitt (often referred to as the "Claw" by players and sports writers) must be seen and tried to be appreciated.

- Trapper design permits mitt to break as much on little finger side as on thumb side.

- Clever design and construction causes both sides of mitt to close over ball when ball hits center panel, forms a positive trap.

- Built in five models (see next page).

Rawlings First Base Mitts Feature—

● GROOVED ACTION PAD	● INNER GREASED PALM
Stiff leather reinforcements set between two layers of padding at thumb, toe and side form a definite groove when player closes his hand, a new original feature that makes trapping the ball very easy. (Standard on all mitts down through our No. B402.)	This treatment of the inside of palm with our newly developed grease gives the leather a firmer texture, keeps mitt feeling firmer and assures smooth pocket through holding pad and palm closer together. (Standard on all mitts down through our No. B402.)

— 16 —

WC—"Walker Cooper" Catchers Mitt with Patented "Deep Well" Laced Pocket. Semi-scoop toe, edge style heel and thumb. Patented palm crotch extension. Pro-Laced U crotch. Cemented back. Improved Nu-Grip streamlined back fitted with adjustable thumb and little finger loops. Made of top quality Tan color cowhide. Hand-formed and shaped felt pad with full break at side allowing for flex at this point. Inner-Greased palm. Roll leather bound edges. Leather laced outer edge. Distinctive ball trap lacing that fits through body of mitt. The cross laces are held in position with Rawlings new "web strain equalizer" and the horizontal part of trap lace is leather wrapped. Patented wrist adjustment and back opening. See opposite page for description and illustrations of Patented "Deep Well" laced pocket.

Trade each $22.95   **List each $30.50**

BE—Bruce Edwards "Target" Baseball Catchers Mitt. A truly modern catchers mitt incorporating the very latest in modern designing features. The "Target" is

Gloves need hinges, and this Walker Cooper Rawlings model sported one in 1953. It would take a few more years before fielders' gloves adapted to this necessity. Courtesy of Rawlings Sporting Goods.

mitt that put protection first and forced a player to catch in a tiny pocket corresponding to his own sore palm. Lou Gehrig's right hand was x-rayed late in his career; it showed evidence of 17 fractures.

As mitts evolved like gloves—losing padding, being oriented on the diagonal, gaining hinges, large webs, and thumbs that helped produce a deep pocket and a firm grip—players could spare their hands. The breakthrough date for first basemen's mitts was 1940, with Rawlings' introduction of the Trapper.

You might scratch your head at why forties fielders' gloves didn't pick up on the Trapper's big web and deep pocket, but that's the way it was. Catchers' mitts entered modernity with hinges and the first big, solid webs in the mid-fifties.

Scratch your head again at why fielders' gloves needed a few more years to grow a hinge.

Early in the 20th century, a catcher's mitt was called "the windpad" and a glove a "hand-shoe." *Handschu* is German for glove.

Why did it take so long for the perfect glove to evolve? Partly it was baseball's natural traditionalism—although this is too vague an answer. That traditionalism, where gloves are concerned, was a product of the manly ethos explained in the previous chapter. Once gloves were accepted, players were still hesitant to let it appear that the glove, rather than the man wearing it, was earning the kudos and the money. "The glove, not the hands, does the work now," Hall of Fame third baseman Pie Traynor, who starred in the twenties and thirties, hissed in 1959.

There was also the fear born of superstition, the dark cloud that trails every pro athlete. If a glove without fingerlaces brought a man to the major leagues, he'd be hesitant to entrust his livelihood to something radically different.

There were business factors as well. Although baseball became a big-money game in the first half of the 20th century, the many companies making equipment remained regional and relatively small. As long as players at all levels—but especially major leaguers—were happy with the gloves they had (and the Bill Doak model was in the Rawlings catalog for 33 years), there was little impetus to change. "There was no marketing advantage in innovation," says John Golomb, a glove historian and custom glovemaker whose family has owned or run the Everlast sports equipment company for decades and has seen tradition at work in boxing. So it is no coincidence

"He did not always catch balls on top of his head, but he could do it in a pinch," wrote John Lardner about Babe Herman, a National League outfielder between the world wars. Sometime teammate Fresco Thompson said of Herman: "He wore a glove for one reason: it was a league custom. The glove would last him a minimum of six years because it rarely made contact with the ball."

that the A2000 came at a time when Wilson and its competitor Rawlings were becoming national sporting goods powerhouses.

This chapter started with a comparison of gloves to airplanes. That comparison is dramatic but not entirely fair. There was much more at stake where planes were concerned. General Billy Mitchell wrote in his 1925 book *Winged Defense*, "It is probable that future war [sic] will be conducted by a special class, the air force, as it was by the armored knights in the Middle Ages." But baseball is a game of peace; in fact, baseball gloves have always been what the U.S. government sends to soldiers overseas for wartime recreation. Why did gloves evolve slowly? Because they could. Good for them and good for us.

There is no proof that major leaguers have ever used their teeth to break in a glove. But they've tried everything else. Here Yankees pitcher Jeff Weaver is merely taking out a little anger on his glove.

Courtesy of AP/Wide World Photos.

CHAPTER **4**

Taming the Beast:
The History of the Break-In, as Told by Major Leaguers

*"It's like gardening. Either you have a green thumb
and it's something you know how to do, or you don't."*

—*Scott Brosius, who won a Gold Glove at third base in 1999*

Breaking in a baseball glove used to be a violent affair. Hot water, cold water, steam, hot air, tobacco spit, baseball bats, scissors, knives, and other gruesome means have been employed by major leaguers. Gloves had been in existence for 90 years before they became truly ergonomic and responsive. Until then, players took a new glove's stubbornness for granted, and glovemakers in turn assumed players wanted to perform their own surgical procedures. Gloves are more agreeable now, and one way to follow the evolution of the glove is to follow the evolution of the break-in. Here's the story from the players themselves—and in a couple of cases from people who were nearby.

In Babe Ruth's day, it seems you almost needed a miracle worker to prepare your glove.

REPORTER WILL WEDGE from the *New York Sun* in 1925:

"The Yankees are fortunate in having one of the best glove doctors in the majors. He is [former major leaguer] Charley O'Leary. . . . He can take a glove that is inclined to buck and shy at grounders and break it in like a Western cowboy and rodeo rider would break in a

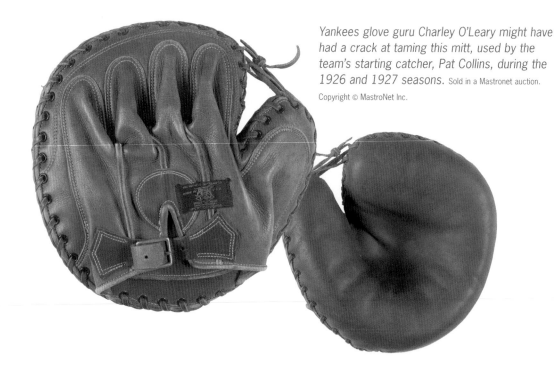

Yankees glove guru Charley O'Leary might have had a crack at taming this mitt, used by the team's starting catcher, Pat Collins, during the 1926 and 1927 seasons. Sold in a Mastronet auction.

Copyright © MastroNet Inc.

bad-tempered bronco. . . . It's said he whispers things into the fingers of stiff and unwieldy gloves that gives them the secret of snaring everything that comes their way. . . . He takes gloves apart and rebuilds them nearer the heart's and fingers' desire. He unlaces the new glove and amputates excess padding. He redistributes the stuffing to points where it will do the most good. He puts Vaseline on the inside of the glove and manipulates it until it is pliable. . . . Sometimes he cuts little circular holes in the palm to make the ball stick better. . . . The fingers of the gloves have to be padded and stiff now to absorb the force of the bad hops of the lively ball that otherwise would cause more fractures than they do. . . . Formerly the frothy juice of the tobacco wad was an important ingredient in the seasoning of a new glove, but the new generation of players is not so keen for the chewing tobacco tanning process. . . . A crude oil shampoo or a Vaseline rub, with a little dash of hair tonic of Glostura to make the ball lay smooth when it gets in the glove, is now the more accepted method. . . . It is really the way Charley talks to a glove and discusses things with it that makes it the dapper and well-groomed object it becomes when he has finished with it. . . . "

Or do it yourself, but don't be delicate about it.

DAVE BANCROFT, one of the best-fielding shortstops of his time, 1915–1930 (as told to Frank Graham in *Baseball Magazine*, February 1932):

"How long since you've seen a player scraping his bat with a piece of glass or polishing it with a bone? How long since you've seen a ballplayer work on his glove?" [Bancroft's break-in:] "Soak it in [a] barrel of water [for a] couple of hours, straighten it out, manipulate and soften the palm and fingers and smooth down the felt lining. . . . Take a ball, put it in the palm and fold the glove over just as it would be folded if I had it on and was gripping the ball. Wind twine around it and tie it tightly to hold it in that form, wrap it in a towel and put it in locker.

The next day unwrap it and begin twisting and rubbing it, then give it a coat of white Vaseline. Rub it in thoroughly. Roll it lengthwise with the thumb inside, wrap it in a damp towel and put it back in my locker. Repeat this every day for about a week, then the glove would be fit to use. A glove treated like that was as effective in snaring the ball as though I had a net strapped [to] my hand. No matter where the ball hit, it would find a pocket and stick. It would take the evil intent out of a bad hop and reduce a savage line drive to a mere putout. It would fill the bill."

In the years leading up to WWII, players still had to do radical surgery.

LEO DUROCHER, who led all National League shortstops in fielding three times between 1925 and 1945 and used only two gloves during that span (from his autobiography, *Nice Guys Finish Last*):

"[Future Hall-of-Fame shortstop Rabbit Maranville] gave me something more tangible than advice, too. A brand-new glove. And then he took a big scissors and cut a hole right in the middle of it, just the way he did with his own glove. You were catching the ball really against the bare skin. It stung like hell at first, but it was

Leo Durocher (left) needed only two gloves during his long playing career; he cut a hole in the first one to bare his palm, but thought better of the idea for the second one, shown here.

From the Rucker Archive.

surprising how quickly my hand hardened. In a very short time, I felt nothing at all except when I'd catch a hot line drive. (The gloves in those days were so much smaller than they are today that you can't really call them the same thing. In those days the player had to make the play, not the glove.)

"I used Rabbit Maranville's glove on through the minors and during my first couple of years with the Yankees. I kept it until it was such a rag that I could fold it up and stuff it in my pocket. When the time finally came when I had to get myself a new one, I picked up a scissors and got ready to cut out another hole. And then I asked myself why. I was doing it because Maranville did it, and that was no reason at all. Instead of cutting a hole in the glove, I slit the inside, took out all the padding and kept a layer of leather between the ball and

Yogi Berra would have put this mitt in the whirlpool "until it stopped bubbling." Then he'd have tossed it in the clubhouse clothes dryer for a few days.
From the Rucker Archive.

my hand. That one was in tatters by the time I was through. It was practically falling apart, but I held onto it to the end of my career. They were the only two gloves I ever had."

By midcentury, there was less violence going on. A dunk in water became the preferred method, followed by various manipulations.

EDDIE JOOST, two-time All-Star shortstop, 1936–1955:

"I'd make sure my glove was not too stiff. The only place I wanted it stiff was in the heel. I'd form the pocket from the heel up to my fingers. In the palm it would be just the leather on my hand, no padding.

We got used to breaking in our gloves. A lot of guys would stick it in a bucket of water. They'd even do that with their shoes. You wanted them to fit tight, perfectly. Sit them in water overnight and the next day, in spring training, put your foot in there and the shoe would form right to your foot. That's how I did it."

YOGI BERRA, 15-time All-Star catcher, 1946–1965:

"Just put [the mitt] in the whirlpool, soak it, until it stopped bubbling. Wrap balls in it with rubber bands. Then dry it out. We used to have a clothes dryer. It was like a heater. Put [the mitt] in there for two or three days."

Ron Santo, five-time Gold Glove–winning third baseman, 1960–1974:

"I would put two baseballs in it, wrap it real tight with string and then put it in water and let it sit all night, take it out the next day and let it dry out. Then I would go play catch with it. And I would keep spitting in it, and after the first day get it kind of soft in the pocket but leave it firm on the outside. Then I'd put oil on it in the pocket."

Then again, some still preferred violent means.

Bill Davis of Lorton, Virginia, glove collector:

Davis was a batboy for the Philadelphia Phillies in the sixties, and a player asked him to break in a glove for him. Davis "was working on it in the dugout when Jim Busby, a coach then of the Astros, came up. He said, 'Kid, let me show you how to break in a mitt.' He then proceeded to pound the daylights out of the glove with a baseball bat."

Methods started becoming gentler 25 years ago—maybe a little water, some steam, or some glove oil.

Ozzie Smith, 13-time Gold Glove–winning shortstop, 1978–1996:

"The softest part had to be the pocket, because that was where all the feel was. I'd take shaving cream with lanolin and rub it in the pocket—that's the part I tried to form the quickest. Shaving cream or baby oil—I never took and used a lot of water. That to me only makes the glove heavy, like sweat. The more you use the glove the more sweat-logged it is and it dries out the leather. When I got done with my glove after a game, I would stick a ball in the pocket to keep the shape."

Robby Thompson, fine defensive second baseman, 1986–1996:

"What I would do is soak it in a hot whirlpool, submerge it a couple minutes, then take it out and start beating and form-ing it like I wanted with the little mallet with the ball on the end. I'd do that 10 or 15 minutes, then take it out on a sunny day and let the sun evaporate the water from it, and I'd be real surprised how broke in it would get. The next couple days you'd use it and it would be real close to ready to use. I would never wrap it up. I wanted the sun to dry it out. I didn't want it to get all beat up like in a dryer, but to dry in the form I wanted it. I broke in a glove in Double A in 1985, and then the next year I made the big-league club and used it for 10 years.

"Now Matt Williams, when a glove got just the littlest bit flimsy, he'd get rid of it. He had such good hands, he'd use that new glove—I don't even think he soaked it, just used it a little bit in pregame and then used it in a game. That'd kill me. There's a man who trusted his hands right there."

RYNE SANDBERG, nine-time Gold Glove–winning second baseman, 1981–1997:

"I used to start off by boiling a pan of water and holding the glove above the steam, and it seemed to soften the leather and break it down a little. After that I'd put shaving cream all over the glove and rub it in. It's another way to moisturize the glove without making it heavy, like glove oil does. I like a glove to stay light. Then I'd do a lot of playing catch in the warm weather."

No oil, no water, nothing fancy: Derek Jeter just plays with a new glove during spring training, and it's ready for one season's use. David Durochik/Sportpics.

BRADY ANDERSON, major league outfielder since 1988:

"I dip a glove in water and then beat it with a bat a little bit, then wrap it around a softball. My dad taught me to do that. I used to submerge it in a tub, now I just run water over it. Rawlings, when they're new, you can't even close them until you work with them, you'd drop every ball. It takes me a couple months until I can use a new glove in a game. Sometimes I'm even forced to use a glove before I want to."

Nowadays gloves are made a bit more supple and ergonomically close to perfect. Break-in is simple and humane.

OMAR VIZQUEL, multiple Gold Glove–winning shortstop, in majors since 1989:

"I just catch a lot of ground balls, I don't like to put oils or shaving cream on it. Some guys tie it up with balls or put it in a microwave, but I don't like any of that. I let it take its regular shape."

JIM THOME, All-Star first baseman, in majors since 1991:

"I just play catch, put a little Lexol [a lanolin-based treatment] or shaving cream on it, just enough to get that little crease out of the palm."

DEREK JETER, All-Star shortstop, in majors since 1995:

"No oil, I just play with it. I use one glove a year. A lot of players use a glove five, eight years, I just basically switch it up each year."

BRANDON INGE, major league catcher since 2001:

"I'll take the end of the bat and pound it right where I want the ball to stick in the pocket. Sometimes I crank up the pitching machine as fast as it goes and take 150 balls. And I'll catch 10 'bullpens' a day. In spring training I can get a mitt ready in two or three days."

Or you can try Rickey Henderson's unique method: A reporter once asked Henderson if a young ballplayer reminded him of himself at a young age. Rickey responded with something like, "Ain't no one reminds Rickey of Rickey except Rickey." Fair enough—Henderson is one of a kind. Once he made a young Rawlings salesman break in his glove. The glove rep was trying hard to get Henderson to switch companies, and Rickey told the guy to break in a glove himself, then he'd try it. The rep spent a frantic several hours kneading a glove and playing catch with a friend, then presented the glove to Rickey. Rickey liked it and signed with Rawlings.

Never one to do it the usual
way, Rickey Henderson
once made a glove salesman
break in his glove.

Ron Vesely/Sportpics.

Please Don't Leave Me

Most major leaguers get all the gloves they need for free. The irony is that often they want only one—forever. Brooks Robinson's glove was hideous, if *The New York Times'* Ira Berkow is to be believed. He described a cracked pocket, ripped insides, dark and shrunken wool padding, a small, dirty piece of tape along the heel and another on the web, the whole thing "a tobacco-juice brown."

Dave Winfield's glove had a hole in the pocket you could see through. So did Chet Lemon's. So did Amos Otis'. Excellent fielders, all of them, yet their gloves were so old, they had the right to veto a trade.

Otis Nixon says, "Mel Hall had the raggediest and ugliest glove I've ever seen in my life. I'd always say you should take care of your tools and equipment,

Brooks Robinson trolled the locker room for gloves to trade his teammates for. When he found a good one, he used it until it was ragged.
From the Rucker Archive.

but his glove was breaking in back and had a shoestring running through the back of it and if you held it up, it would just fold back. He had a name for it. I can't remember that. But the manager made him change gloves." Was Hall like that in the rest of his life? "I don't want to get into that," Nixon says.

Robinson and teammate Willie Miranda would put tongue depressors in the fingers of their gloves to keep them firm. Robby Thompson slathered pine tar inside the palm to achieve the same thing.

Current utility infielder Kevin Jordan describes the Alan Trammell model SSK he wore for nine years, from high school to the majors: "The back part under the web tore, so my dad took an old piece of leather and glued it there and took

sidebar continued on next page

Travis Fryman wore a Zett glove, from Japan, and cared for it as the Japanese do: regular cleanings and light oilings. That's a rarity in American locker rooms. David Durochik/Sportpics.

fishing line to string it up. And when the thumb loop tore, I put a piece of leather there and Super Glued it along with some fishing line, and it lasted another four years." Jordan's a glove lover. He never throws out an old glove and still has the web of his Little League model in a special pouch in his locker along with needles and fishing line and other glove-repair stuff.

But to be truthful, raggedy gloves are the exception, not the rule. Some players are downright meticulous. Travis Fryman wiped down his last gamer, a five-year-old Zett, once a week and applied a little Glove Loogie lanolin oil on it each time. The glove was dark and shiny from the oil yet still strong after thousands of grounders. He made a study of gloves and says Japanese-made, like his Zett, are "second to none."

And for glove care, Japanese players are second to none. "You should treat a glove like a child," the famous Japanese glove designer Yoshii Tsubota told a reporter. "You should put some oil in it every time after using it. Not too much, just a little, spread it around." Tsubota works for Mizuno and earned the country's Emperor's Award for excellence as a craftsman a few years ago. He makes Ichiro Suzuki's gloves, and recently at an All-Star Game Ichiro was walking along the waterfront to the private boat he'd rented. A throng of fans followed him. He crossed paths with Tsubota—and bowed to him.

Bill Mazeroski had no Tsubota. In his day many ballplayers found shoe repair-men to fix their gloves. One near Forbes Field "knew my gloves well," Mazeroski said. But Phil Rizzuto sent his to the Rawlings factory. "He probably played 14 years with the same glove. At least he looked on it as being the same glove," says Roger Lueckenhoff, a Rawlings glove executive for 42 years, until 1993. "[Glove designer] Harry Latina would refurbish it every year and replace parts, and he kept gradually replacing parts to where it was a new glove, but in Rizzuto's mind it was the same glove. He's the only player I knew of who had that superstition."

Well, Walt Weiss had a similar one. Weiss' glove was old and floppy. Once the

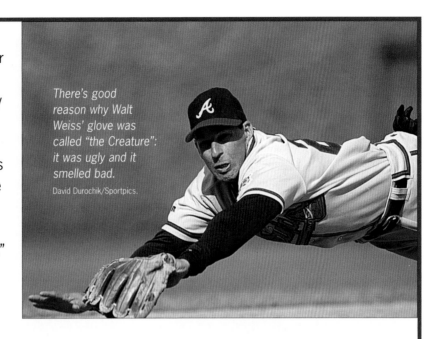

There's good reason why Walt Weiss' glove was called "the Creature": it was ugly and it smelled bad.
David Durochik/Sportpics.

back strap ripped right off, and out of respect for Weiss and his glove, a Rawlings glove repairman fixed it that day, even though Weiss' glove was a Mizuno. Its nickname was "the Creature," for good reason. Plug your nose and read this from California Angels' trainer Tom Probst, who also did a little work on Weiss' glove: "I've dealt with saddles and

stuff like that, and in the later years they get what's called dry rot, where the leather is just rotting away and it becomes brittle, and if you try to put oil in a dry-rotted saddle you pick up a smell, and that was very similar to picking up Walt's glove. You couldn't tell by holding it in hand, but later on your hands would have that smell."

A kid's first glove should be inexpensive and measure eight or nine inches from heel to fingertips, like this $28.60 Ken Griffey model (top). By the time he or she has reached the age of 12, an 11½-incher is just fine—nearly adult size. This Derek Jeter model has a list price of $58.60. Courtesy of Rawlings Sporting Goods.

CHAPTER 5

Major Milestone:
Helping a Youngster Buy the Right Glove

*"In our clinic, we joke that you need to stay away from
any glove with 'Big Anything' in the name."*

—*Al Price, coauthor of* The Official Little League Education Program

When the little ballplayer is ready for a real game of catch—around age four or five—he or she is ready for a real glove. Here's the expert wisdom on buying the right glove for a youngster.

Youth baseball coaches say a real glove has a palm made of leather or good synthetic leather. Plastic or cheap vinyl is fine on the back for a beginner, but on the front, those materials crack or tear quickly. Glovemakers shouldn't even bother shipping those gloves to the States. Look for the words "genuine leather" or "synthetic leather" on a glove. It needn't cost more than $30.

Almost all gloves these days state their size somewhere on the pinkie or thumb. Look for one between eight and ten inches long for kids between ages five and eight, favoring one on the small side.

Compare several gloves and look for one that's light. And look for one that's soft. Why? "At this age, catching is really a 'catch-and-cover-up thing,' learning how to use two hands," says Al Price, a veteran kids' coach and coauthor of *The Official Little League Education Program*. "There's variation in the sizes of kids, but most just don't have a lot of hand and arm strength at this age."

Tempting as they are, stay away from the newfangled gloves with the deep, over-sized webs. Price says these encourage kids to spear the ball with one hand and to rely on the web when they should be learning to catch the ball at the ideal spot, in the pocket just below the index finger, where there's most room for error and from where it's easier to retrieve the ball. Well-trained ballplayers need the web only when they've misjudged a ball or are stretching for a hot shot.

Look closely at web, palms, and fingers. Relatively speaking, you want a glove with more palm and less finger and web. "Theoretically you should be able to play catch without a web," Price says. In fact, some youth-league coaches have their kids play catch with webless gloves and tennis balls to hone this skill. Others lend the kids old-fashioned gloves with stubby fingers and no laces between them, so that they have to rely on the palm, as Honus Wagner and Babe Ruth and Pee Wee Reese did. (So, by the way, do Omar Vizquel and Bret Boone today, because they're so good.)

And you want the pocket to be shallow. "In a shallow glove, the ball is always available," Price says. "And it's very seldom in baseball or softball that you don't follow up a catch with a throw. In a deep glove, the ball just disappears and the kids end up taking extra steps and fishing for the ball."

Buy all-leather gloves for kids over 8 years old. For 9- and 10-year-olds, a 10½-inch glove is as big as it should get. A 12-year-old can usually handle an 11½-inch glove. These suggestions apply to boys and girls both, as there's usually little difference in hand size until puberty sets in. Err on the small side, however, if you suspect a child is still lacking in hand and arm strength.

Detroit played rookie Roy Johnson in the outfield in 1929; he led the league with 45 doubles but made an astonishing 31 errors. One day after he dropped a routine fly, manager Bucky Harris said, "Forget it kid, the ball hit you in a bad spot—the middle of your glove."

Kids at most ages feel bigger is better, so be prepared to do a little negotiating. "It works to remind an older kid that a lot of major leaguers use an 11½-inch glove," Price says. Overall, he adds, half of all youth players are lugging around gloves that are too big for them.

There are two innovations Price does endorse: the thin, dense foam or gel pads sewn into palms, and the various new wrist straps that snug a glove a little tighter. A bone bruise doesn't encourage a kid to keep catching at the base of the index finger, so Price views the pads as "an awesome development."

The snugger device makes a kid more nimble with his or her glove and more confident. Just make sure it is not overtight, as this will hinder the hand as it tries to squeeze the glove closed.

And Price doesn't object to a youngster wearing a thin batting glove under the glove or putting the index finger out of the glove, as the pros do. This works to protect the finger, and there's a second benefit: when the index finger's out of the way, the other three can close the glove more commandingly toward the thumb.

By the time a boy reaches 13 or 14, he can use a major league–size glove, even a 12¾-inch outfielder's model. The same goes for a girl softballer, assuming she's strong enough and the glove is on the light side. She'll need the extra leather to handle the bigger ball.

There's another milestone around this age. A baseball player can start using a mitt at first base. Price recommends a regular fielders' glove before this age, to encourage catching in the right spot. First basemen's mitts have big webs, and this can encourage bad habits in a younger player.

Once a youngster has a glove, he or she will want to oil it. Kids are notorious overoilers, so Price follows many glovemakers in suggesting shaving cream with lanolin for that exciting break-in experience. Lanolin is considered the best leather treatment around. Now, shaving cream is mostly soap, and soap's not the best thing for leather. But shaving cream is so light and airy, it's almost impossible to overuse it anywhere, except on Dad's face while he's sleeping.

A little glove oil and a lot of catch are all you really need to break in a glove. But this $25 mallet from Texas glovemaker Nokona (left) speeds the process, one reason why teams from the Little Leagues to the major leagues use it. Or, if you're handy with tools, you can make something like the mallet on the right with a ball, a dowel, a long lag screw, a large washer, and a couple of drill bits. David Durochik/Sportpics.

CHAPTER 6

Getting to Know You: Breaking in Your Glove

"I bathed it in oil (Rawlings glove oil, I believe), tied a string around it (with a ball in the pocket), and put it under some books to help develop the pocket. Several days later, I went out to play with the 'big guys' and never let the glove out of my sight."

—David Stern, NBA commissioner, on breaking in his first glove

If you're old enough to remember the little argument George Brett and Billy Martin had over pine tar on a bat, you're old enough to have enjoyed breaking in a glove. It was a sluggish process and it tried the patience. When you thought you had them, balls mocked you and popped out. So you added more oil, pounded the glove again, and played more ball. By midseason it was better than fine, and you were proud. *That was kind of fun*, you thought.

So when did breaking in a new baseball glove stop being fun?

The 21st century has little affection for a slow job done well. All sorts of newfangled glove softeners are available. One advertises that it has "solved the problem" of breaking in a glove. In fact, you're not obligated to break in a new glove at all now. "Pre-broken-in" or "ready-to-play" gloves abound, known in the business as "trunk-slammers" because you can buy one at lunch, pull it out of your trunk that evening, slam the trunk, and the glove is ready to go.

There's a trade-off here. It's baseball's version of the conflict, described by Freud, between the pleasure and reality principles. You can buy a ready-to-play glove and love it the minute you use it, but you won't love it forever. After a season or two of hard play, it will be a rag. Or you can buy an old-fashioned stiff glove and grapple with it for a few months, and it will last nearly forever. Tighten all the laces every season or two and it'll be as good as the day you declared it broken-in—maybe even better, because it will remember everything your hand ever asked it to be.

That's the problem with ready-to-play gloves: they don't mold to your hand very much or for very long. In order to be pliable right off the rack, they have to be made with thinner, softer, oilier leathers. These gloves lose their shape faster and never regain it. The laces—which are like the skeleton of a glove—are thinner and stretchier too. And the padding is literally spongier. Think of a sponge. It flexes happily along with your hand, and then it forgets your hand and returns to its original shape. So a ready-to-use glove is never really *yours*. There's a saying: "Men love women, women love children, children love hamsters, and hamsters love no one." Ready-to-use gloves are like hamsters . . . with logos.

In a more traditional glove, the leather is thicker and denser. It's not heavily lubricated with oils at the tannery, and its padding contains more dense wool or synthetic wool, which conforms gradually but

forever to the contours of your palm and your fingers.

So pick the glove that suits you. Need it fast? Don't play much? Buying it for a son or daughter who will outgrow it in a season or two? Don't have much patience with inanimate objects? Go squishy and don't feel guilty.

Are you a good player? Is this "the last glove you'll ever buy"? Do you like putting off a little gratification now for a lot later? Then buy a nice stiff glove and get to work. Either way, congratulate yourself for not having bought a video game.

A confession: there's no law saying you have to do anything to a new glove except play with it. If you're in no big rush or you're a serious player playing ball every day, let the glove break in naturally, just kneading it with your throwing hand between pitches. Many perfectly good major leaguers—Omar Vizquel, Derek Jeter, and Mark Grace, to name a few—do this. But major leaguers have the advantage of long, hot spring trainings and major league throws to soften up their gloves.

Still, if you're eager, here's a safe, effective, and quick way to break in yours. It's the same process for a trunk-slammer or a traditional glove; just repeat as necessary. But don't oil any new glove more than once.

* Put a game on the television, then look at your glove. Does it look or say "pre-oiled"? If so, don't use another drop of oil on it. If not, put a very light coating of glove oil everywhere, front and back, and then forget about the fingers and thumb until next year. Gloves are not overly dry right off the rack, according to Paul Storch, a leather expert at the Minnesota Historical Society and a slow-pitch softball third baseman. "It's a myth that leather needs to be fed and moisturized," he says. New gloves are just stiff, and a little bit of oil lubricates the thousands upon thousands of little leather fibers so they slide against each other more easily. (Which glove oil? Or maybe something else entirely? See the sidebar on page 62.)

David Durochik/Sportpics.

The glove shown here and on the previous page is a top-of-the-line model from U.S. maker Glovesmith, which makes the majority of its gloves in a small but busy Missouri plant. Only Texas-based Nokona makes a higher percentage of its gloves—all of them—in the United States. David Durochik/Sportpics.

Next go to work on the catching zone.

* Put another light coating of glove oil at the hinge, in an area the size of a golf ball. ❶ Do it on both sides, front and back, and make sure you don't miss the layers of piping and the laces on the edge. There are eight or more layers of

leather at the hinge, counting the piping, and it's the stubbornest spot on a glove.

* Add another very light coat of oil in the pocket, from the hinge all the way up to the web. ❷ Then add a bit more to the web, front and back, hitting the laces that encircle the top. ❹

Now the fun starts.

* Whale on it, right in the catching zone. ❸ Sit down, watch the Chicago Cubs leave runners on base, and pound a ball into the pocket right where you want to catch it. Or do as the pros sometimes do: put it on the grass and pound the fat end of a bat where you want the pocket to be, especially if you're a catcher or first base-

man. In his book *Baseball My Way*, Hall of Fame second baseman Joe Morgan wrote, "If you have a genuine leather glove, you can . . . do just about anything you want with it. You can beat it. You can take the barrel end of a bat and pound down into the pocket to soften the leather, or to make the pocket as large or as small as you want." At one point in his

[**QUICK GUIDE**] To Breaking It In

- Put a game on the TV. Turn down the sound and tune in the radio broadcast.

- Put a very light coating of glove oil everywhere on your glove.

- Put another light coating of oil at the hinge, in an area the size of a golf ball. ❶ Do it on both sides, front and back, and make sure you don't miss the layers of piping and the laces on the edge.

- Add another light coat of oil in the pocket, from the hinge all the way up to the web. ❷ Then add a bit more to the web, front and back, hitting the laces that encircle the top. ❹

- Whale on it right in the catching zone with a ball or the fat end of a bat or a glove mallet. ❸ Unless the glove's a cheapie, it'll stand up to everything you give it.

- Hit it at other tough spots: the front and back of the web, the top of the web, the backside where the web meets the pocket, and the fingertips. ❼

- Knead the web and hinge in your fingers until one or the other cries uncle. Give lots of attention to the stiff area where the web is laced to the pocket. ❺

- Put your hands on the back of the glove and pinch the leather closed here, as if you're catching a marble in the pocket. ❻ Do this until you're really bored.

- Close the glove the way you want it to close, lay it on the ground, and pound down on the closed hinge to loosen up the leather, the laces, and the tightly sewn thread. ❶

- Turn off the TV and the radio. Go outside and play a lot of catch, closing your hand around the ball in the way—vertical or horizontal—that shapes the glove to suit your hand and your position.

- Between throws, keep shaping the glove with your throwing hand.

- Repeat the above steps as necessary, but don't oil again.

- You know your glove's broken in when you're going for a tough backhand and the ball hits your glove at the very base of the palm and sticks, even though you couldn't get a firm grip on your own.

career, Morgan had used only three gloves in 15 years, so you can trust him that a good glove will take the pounding.

* Knead the web and hinge in your fingers until one or the other cries uncle. Give lots of attention to the stiff area where the web is laced to the pocket. ❺ Put your hands on the back of the glove and pinch the leather closed there, as if you're catching a marble in the pocket. ❻ Do this until you're really bored.

* Do you like gadgets? Buy a handsome, lathe-turned wooden mallet from the Texas glove company Nokona and hammer away at the pocket, the hinge, the web, everywhere. (Call 800-433-0957 for a dealer.) Smack the pocket ❸ and the web. ❹ Hit down on the web and the fingertips from above. ❼ And here's a key move: close the glove the way you want it to close, lay it on the ground, and bring the mallet down on the closed hinge to loosen up the leather, the laces, and the tightly sewn thread. ❶

Sounds violent, but most major league clubs use several such mallets in different sizes. When Pittsburgh Pirates catcher Jason Kendall has a new glove, he turns it over to equipment man Roger Wilson for a good pounding. If your glove's good, it'll survive the mallet easily and last until you outgrow it. Or until you get mad at it and throw it in the stands, as Kerry Wood of the Chicago Cubs did during one rotten outing.

* Pounding it and kneading it will soften up the glove and start to make it playable. But it won't make it yours. Using it will. Play a lot of catch. Try to catch the ball where you'll always want it. (Experts say you should catch the ball just below the glove's first finger, where the whole glove can fold around it. But top infielders often catch it lower in the palm, and outfielders and catchers tend to like it a little higher up.) And while you're giving the glove a pocket this way, it's learning where you like your hand to be—deep inside the glove as some major league infielders like it, or farther out on your fingertips, as many outfielders do.

So you can't overwork the pocket. "The softest part has to be the pocket. That's where all the feeling is," says 13-time Gold Glover Ozzie Smith. But shape and break are vital too. They help the glove do the job for your position. Here are some tips for gloves at each position:

Outfielders prefer their gloves long and narrow, like the top glove on the left, and broken in so that the thumb and pinkie come together around the ball. Infielders like a glove that's shorter and wider, as below, with a thumb and index finger that close together around the ball.

These two models, made by America (above) and Guerrero, show the Mexican style of glovemaking. Black is the predominant color, as the black dye covers up flaws in otherwise fine leather. (And Mexican leather tends to be good and inexpensive because of more lax environmental laws for tanneries.) Mexican gloves also tend to be vibrant, with brown, white, red, or orange highlights. It's the fashion among Latin players both north and south of the border.

Perceptive readers will note that these gloves are modeled closely on classic Rawlings models whose patents have expired. There's a lot of copying in the glove business, by companies both in the U.S. and abroad. David Durochik/Sportpics.

Outfield: Ninety percent of major league outfielders wear a longer glove, 12 ¾ inches long. (Outfielders under the age of 13 should have a smaller glove, between 10 and 12 ¼ inches, depending on how old they are.)

The pros break them in to be long and relatively skinny—vertical, as they say. They want that extra few inches of length to reach fly balls after a long run or to scoop a rolling ball out of the grass. So they close the glove by bringing their thumb and pinkie together.

Outfielders also want a deep pocket, because they want every ball to stay in there. They're less concerned about making a quick throw than infielders are. That's why many top outfielders (Bernie Williams of the Yankees, for example) put two fingers in the pinkie hole and move the other fingers over so there's nothing in the index finger

hole. This allows them to close the glove even more powerfully while on a dead run. Many of these players began doing this as youngsters.

Second base and shortstop: These players wear a shorter glove, between 10½ and 11½ inches in the major leagues. (Very young players might need a slightly smaller glove than this. But some Pony League and high school players actually like one just a little bigger, maybe 12 inches, until they're at the top of their game.) Most major league middle infielders break in their gloves to be wide and short—"horizontal," they say—by closing them "index finger to thumb." Where an outfielder brings his pinkie to his thumb to create a deep pocket, the middle infielder pinches his thumb and index finger together to create a wider, shallower pocket. That makes it easier to find the ball and make a quick throw. Some infielders go even further, allowing the laces at the tips of the fingers to loosen over time until the fingers fan out, a quarter-inch or more apart. Others do something similar by training the

thumb and pinkie to curve slightly outward. This practice has become common in the past few years, and it looks odd to the George Brett/pine tar crowd, who learned to curve the thumb and pinkie inward. And the whole thing seems odd to anyone who remembers using a glove without laces in the fingertips before the fifties. These ballplayers broke in the glove so the first two or three fingers curved downward, making a kind of cup. To each his own, said the old lady as she kissed her cow.

Third base: Third base mixes outfield and infield. Here the most important thing is gloving the ball, as third basemen usually have ample time to throw. So they often use a midsized glove—12 inches is the average for pros and good college or high school players. (There are exceptions, naturally. Robin Ventura's glove is huge, closer to 12¾ inches, like an outfielder's. Travis Fryman, a former shortstop, used a compact 11½-inch glove.) They break in the glove with a deeper pocket than a shortstop would and with a more "vertical" shape. "I wanted the

When Microsoft owner Bill Gates was nine, he had a formal contract with his sister giving him the rights to use her baseball glove in exchange for $5.

Jason Kendall is one of many catchers who break their mitt in "over the top," with the fingertip area curved downward.

David Durochik/Sportpics.

confidence to reach a hard smash with the web if I had to," says five-time Gold Glover Ron Santo.

First base: First basemen's mitts are a mixture too. Most want the palm and web extremely soft and flexible, so a short hop to the backhand side sticks there. But they want the thumb and finger area rock hard, so the glove doesn't twist or bend when they catch a ball slightly off the pocket. Eleven-time Gold Glover Keith Hernandez would

tighten the two rows of laces at the finger-tips as tight as they'd go, then wet this area and let the glove dry. He says he wanted it "like reinforced concrete." Find your own preference, but if soft bounces aren't stick-ing and hard throws are overpowering your fingers, you need to keep working on your mitt.

Catcher: Catchers' mitts used to look a lot like first basemen's mitts, and they still do similar work, standing up to burners

Vaseline vs. Saddle Soap vs. Neat's-foot vs....

With every new glove comes the urge to oil it. Go ahead, especially if you want to break it in a little quicker. But be picky about what you use, and be sparing. Here are some tips on oils and other break-in methods.

Not good:

- *Petroleum jelly.* This isn't called an oil because it isn't an oil. Technically, it's a wax. Contrary to what some glove people say, it doesn't allow leather to breathe. It forms a coating, doesn't penetrate the leather, and attracts dust and dirt.

- *Mink oil.* Like good glove oils, this is made from animals, not petroleum, but because it's a paste at room temperature, it resists penetrating the leather. Some glove aficionados suggest you slather a glove in mink oil and heat it in the dryer inside a pillow case. This works, but then the mink oil hardens up again inside the pores.

- *Saddle soap.* This isn't an oil; it's a true soap. Its pH is high, as it's meant to clean a surface and be washed away entirely. But it's likely to penetrate a glove somewhat, where the pH will eventually make the fibers brittle and break. And if the glove ever gets wet, an off-white goo will materialize on the surface and you'll have to buff it out. What a drag.

- *Linseed oil.* Leather experts call this a "drying oil." It forms a film, and if there's a lot of it, it will bond with itself or "cross-link" over time, making the glove stiff. Linseed oil is good for priming wood—not baseball gloves.

- *Household oil, motor oil, bicycle grease, etc.* Heavy, nasty, and permanent.

- *The microwave.* This will really heat up one side of your glove: the inside. If you wouldn't do this to your cat, you don't want to do it to your glove.

So-so:

- *A conventional oven.* There are several new products that claim to break in your glove in a flash—just slather on the product, bake the glove in the oven for a few minutes, then mold it. Some leather experts shudder at the thought of tenderizing a glove this way, but the products do boast credible testimonials.

- *Shaving cream.* There's conflicting evidence here. Scads of major leaguers put a dollop of Gillette Foamy on their gloves. The product is supplied to every major league locker room, and for decades players have assumed the lanolin in it would help soften their gloves. But glove manufacturers disagree. Bob Clevenhagen, who has been designing major league gloves for Rawlings for 26 years, says, "It might make it feel good for a little bit, but it doesn't do any good." Longtime Wilson executive Al Oldenburg said the company used to recommend shaving cream for its new gloves only because it knew kids couldn't overuse the fluffy stuff, as they could neat's-foot oil. And finally, a Gillette spokeswoman notes, "To my knowledge, there's never been lanolin in Foamy."

- *Water.* Use at your own risk. It won't kill a glove, as gloves get caught in the rain all the time and survive. Water or steam causes leather fibers to separate and relink when they dry, an effective but harsh way to shape a glove quickly. Some major leaguers still use a little water—but remember, they get their gloves for free.

- *Spit.* The moisture will soften a glove for molding. Museum people call spit

sidebar continued on next page

a "mild enzymatic solution" because it's actually not a bad cleaner, and someone once researched creating an "artificial saliva." But it'll stiffen up the glove ultimately—Cookie Rojas used copious amounts to keep his ancient glove hard.

- *Coffee, cream, and sugar.* Eddie Brinkman said it worked for him.

Better:

- *Neat's-foot oil.* Formerly made of the oil that rises when you boil cows' hooves, it's now plain old lard that's been treated with sulfuric acid. It penetrates the leather and lubricates well. But use it sparingly. It's heavy, and it darkens leather. If overapplied, it'll make your glove floppy. And if the glove goes unused for a long time, the oil cross-links and the glove gets petrified. (More than one glove collector has stared at a vintage Rawlings Mickey Mantle MM3 and imagined the hundreds it would be worth if someone hadn't slathered it in neat's-foot before leaving it in a hot attic for 40 years.) Many commercial glove treatments use neat's-foot, sometimes mixed with lanolin. Neat's-foot gives

while finessing all sorts of hops. You want a big, soft pocket and no resistance from the hinge. A few major leaguers like a small, tight web, but many others prefer one big and loose enough to snag a foul tip on its own, when it gets there before they're ready. (A few years ago, when Yankees catcher Jorge Posada was discussing webs with Yankees Hall of Famer Yogi Berra, Berra almost got Posada to use the soft, fishnet lace web he'd used in the fifties, shown on pg. 39.) Different catchers like different shapes. Some like a wider glove that breaks more horizontally or "over the top," like a middle infielder's. You'll see these catchers bending the fingertip area of the glove down between pitches. Others, often the ones with longer hands, prefer a longer mitt with a "vertical" break. For them it's more comfortable and gives them more gripping power.

a glove a slightly tacky feel, which some players like.

Best:

- *Lanolin.* Made from the oil in sheep's wool, lanolin is light, it penetrates well, it doesn't stain much, and it lubricates nicely. It stays liquid, which is a problem only if you over-apply it. A favorite lanolin-based product is Lexol (lexol.com), which many glove-makers recommend and lots of pros use. Its minor drawback is that it leaves a dry slipperiness on the leather until there's a little dust on the surface. Regular Lexol doesn't have any of neat's-foot's nice tackiness; try Lexol *nf*—a lanolin/neat's-foot mixture —if you want the better features of both. A newer lanolin product, Glove Loogie (gloveloogie.com), has a bit of the tackiness of neat's-foot oil— it might be the best glove oil available today. It's a favorite of the Cleveland Indians except for Omar Vizquel, who uses nothing.

David Durochik/Sportpics.

Pitcher: Most pitchers' gloves are mid-sized, with solid webs to hide the ball and the fingertips of the throwing hand. These gloves need to handle smashes and grounders of all kinds along with tricky soft tosses from first basemen. Pros tend to make the pocket soft and the web medium-soft while keeping the fingers firm to prevent the glove from flexing and tipping pitches as they adjust their grip on the ball.

You may think you know the answer to this, but just in case: when do you know a glove is broken in? If you're going for a tough backhand and the ball hits the pocket at the very base of the palm and sticks, even though you mistimed it or couldn't get a firm grip on your own, then you know it's broken in. It's doing the job for you.

One Glove's **Brush with** World Affairs

Don't try Merritt Clifton's break-in strategy unless you have nerves of steel. Clifton is the editor of *Animal People* magazine, which covers animal protection issues. He is a member of the Society for American Baseball Research (SABR), and this originally appeared on SABR's informative listserv:

There are all sorts of ways to break in a glove, of course, and I've tried a lot of them. However, one fine day in 1987 I stopped at the post office on my way to play for Richford against Newport, Vermont, and picked up two important items: a desperate note from my friend Eva in Brazil informing me that her work as a volunteer medic working with street children had made her the target of a death squad and wondering if I could intercede with anyone influential to get her into the U.S. or Canada, and a brand-new baseball glove I'd ordered by mail. I put on the stiff-as-a-board glove, with no break-in whatever, took the mound, and with my mind in Brazil proceeded to get shelled for seven runs in three innings.

Relieved and switched to left field, still with my mind elsewhere, I next made the greatest long-running, diving catch of my life to flag down an apparent surefire triple with the bases loaded, threw out a runner on the same play to end the inning, and went 4-for-5 at bat with four RBIs to lead a comeback victory, playing on autopilot.

A whole lot of us did manage to get Eva out of danger, though she went back to Brazil about five years later and I haven't heard from her since.

But about the glove: all the next week I worked off nervous tension by working the leather with oil while contacting everyone I could think of who might be able to help Eva. (Former Canadian prime minister Joe Clark distinguished himself by jumping right in.)

Then, come Sunday and word that she'd probably be safe, I started in center field in a Newport rematch with a beautifully broken-in glove—and, fully concentrating, proceeded to let a fly ball bounce out of it with the bases loaded, after which I kicked the ball about 40 feet off my knee for a three-base error.

It was almost as embarrassing as the time I was playing a deep shortstop and a hockey player named Don Nelson caromed a line drive off my forehead and over a shallow center-field fence for a home run. My brother was pitching and, 30 years later, still reminds me of it about once a week.

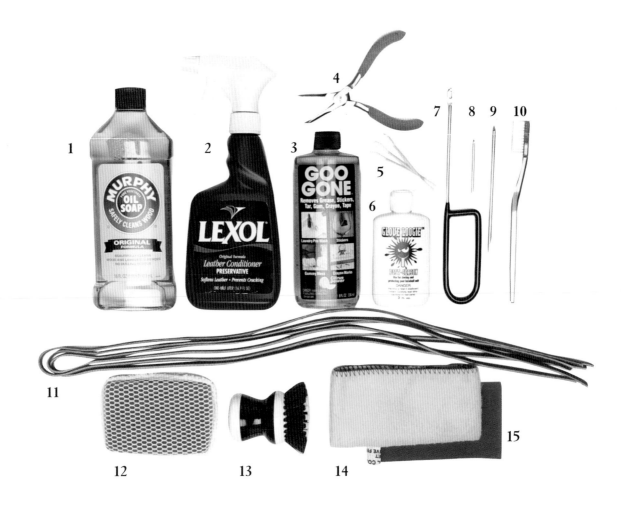

{ FIGURE I }

With a little time you can revive even the dirtiest, flimsiest old glove.
Here are the tools you'll need for any kind of tune-up on every kind of glove. David Durochik/Sportpics.

CHAPTER **7**

Keeping It Tight:
Maintaining Your Glove

*"I cried when I threw out my old A2000. My wife was there; she can verify it.
I didn't know you could fix up an old glove. So I just tossed it out. Man."*

—a 37-year-old Evanston, Illinois, resident

Major leaguers are pretty good at taking care of their gloves. Players will wipe them off when they get dirty and have the equipment manager tighten the laces when they get floppy. A few clean their gloves once a week and apply a little glove oil, as Travis Fryman did. Japanese ballplayers are downright obsessive, many cleaning and oiling their gloves after every game.

Recreational players are just the opposite. Have you ever cleaned your glove? Have you oiled it since you first got it? Tightened or replaced the laces? Nothing says you have to do any of those things. If your 10-year-old glove seems just fine, then use it in good health. But consider what a little maintenance can do. Brushing the dust and dirt off a glove and cleaning it with Murphy's Oil Soap can help the leather last longer, especially inside, where sweat and salt from your palm might be chewing away at the leather at this very moment. A little bit of glove oil in the pocket can keep the leather soft and a bit tacky, as many major leaguers like it. Tightening the laces can work miracles. This will firm up your glove and restore its shape. If you find it's getting hard to pluck a slow roller off the grass or to find the ball in the pocket for a quick throw, your glove's too floppy. It happens to every glove sooner or later.

So here are tips on maintaining all your gloves—even the collectibles you keep on your shelf.

Maintaining a Glove You Use

* Brush all the loose dust and dirt off the outside. Use a brush with lots of soft bristles, like an O-Cedar dish brush (figure 1, item 13). A soft-bristle tooth-brush is good for little seams and crevices (figure 1, item 10). Do this thoroughly, as you want as little dirt as possible on the glove when you wet it in the next step.

* Make a light solution of Murphy's Oil Soap (figure 1, item 1) and water and wash the glove thoroughly with a soft cotton rag or a soft scrubber sponge (figure 1, items 14 and 12). Glove experts and even museum curators suggest Murphy's, as it's made of gentle vegetable oil, not a petroleum product.

Chances are there are spots where the dirt is black and gummy and doesn't want to come off. Work these a little harder, letting the soap and water do

their part. Hit them with the toothbrush too, but go easy.

Pay special attention to the inside of your glove. Sweat'll kill a glove much sooner than the dust that accumulates outside. Many gloves are retired when the insides are all "chafed" and "checked" even though the outsides are still in great shape. Slide the rag way up the thumb and finger holes.

Stop cleaning when you're not getting any more dirt on the rag.

* Let the glove dry overnight. Otherwise you might trap the water in the leather when you oil it and spend the next year wiping off a gummy white film.

* The next day, see if the leather looks bleached and overdry. It's hard for leather to truly dry out. Leather is very porous, and it naturally absorbs and sheds moisture all the time to keep what experts call its "equilibrium moisture content." So your glove will regulate itself unless it's left in a damp basement to rot or mildew or a hot, dry attic to harden.

What can happen to leather, however, is that some of the oils added in the tanning process can leach out if the glove has repeatedly been wetted by your palm or by rain and then dried out, or as the oils bind with dirt and dust and are washed away with your soap and water. The glove will then look pale and dry, and it probably needs a bit of oil.

* Use a lanolin-based oil, and go lightly. Glove oils have been around since at least 1915, when glove companies began using stiffer, chrome-tanned cowhides rather than vegetable-tanned buckskins and other soft leathers that had been fine for work and fashion gloves. Neat's-foot oil was long the favorite. In 1951, the *Official Encyclopedia of Baseball* stated: "If repeated wetting occurs, harshness in the leather may develop, but this can be counter-acted by applying neat's-foot oil or light paraffin (mineral) oil." Neat's-foot, originally derived from the hooves of calves, was such a miracle substance that even libraries and museums applied it over and over again to centuries-old leather bookbindings. Nowadays, pure neat's-foot is out of favor. To their horror, the libraries discovered that neat's-foot discolors leather over time, and it can oxidize, or cross-link, with itself and harden if there's too much of it. Today they use oil sparingly and obsess over humidity levels instead. Libraries and

glove experts like lanolin now, and two good sources of it are Lexol (figure 1, item 2), a general leather treatment available at any hardware store, or Glove Loogie (if you can get past the name), available at gloveloogie.com (figure 1, item 6). If you don't want to spend the money and you've got a tin of neat's-foot hanging around, go ahead and use it—a light annual treatment won't hurt. But go easy. Apply any oil sparingly, because you don't want to weigh down the glove or make it slippery or floppy.

Maintaining a Collectible Glove

* Clean the glove as outlined in the first three steps for maintaining a glove you'd use. Because this one is a glove you're going to display—and if you're a bit meticulous—you might want to try harder to get rid of the caked-on, greasy dirt. Try a solvent like Goo Gone (figure 1, item 3) or grain alcohol dabbed on a Q-Tip (figure 1, item 5), but go easy and experiment on the inside of the glove first, to check for bleaching. Hit these spots with Murphy's Oil Soap the minute you finish with the solvent, to wash away

the extra. Avoid touching any stampings done with ink, such as endorsement signatures.

* Ink stains or the unwanted signatures of the glove's former owner? Use the black, silicon carbide sandpaper starting with the extra fine, 320-grit type (figure 1, item 15). Wet it with a little nonstaining glove oil, like Lexol, to soften the pores and add a bit of safe solvent to the mix. Then go very lightly with the sandpaper, as it's likely you'll take off a little of the leather grain. It's hard to remove ink entirely. Sometimes ink is a part of the glove's past that you can't undo.

* When the glove is completely dry again, polish it and/or dye it if you want to revive the color. To revive it, experienced collectors recommend a liquid Meltonian tinted polish, which contains dye but also has oils that seem to activate the old dyes in the glove. Don't use a paste wax or polish.

Orange- and burgundy-colored gloves revive the best. Lighter, tan gloves are tougher to match for color, especially because the polish often shows darker on the gloves than in the containers. On "blond" gloves, use "banana" or neutral tints. Pre-1920 green gloves are hard to match. Just be proud you own such an interesting specimen.

If you like the results of your polishing, buff the glove lightly but thoroughly. It should be ready to display.

* If the glove's color is mottled or the leather seems bleached and you're willing to take a little risk, dye it, using Lincoln or Fiebing's products. Tandy dyes seem to lack power, the glove experts say. Once it's dyed and dry, polish the glove with a Meltonian polish.

"Don Buford worked for Sears, Roebuck in the winter time, and they came out with these red gloves and green gloves," says Brooks Robinson. "The damn things were as hard as rocks. Buford was a terrific player but a little shaky in the outfield, and we ended up calling them the Stop Glove and the Go Glove [respectively]. The green glove was the hardest, and a couple times the ball hit it and bounced out over the fence. We told [Buford] to keep the Go Glove on the bench."

{ FIGURE 2 }

Laces are the skeleton of a glove. A 10-minute tightening can make your glove better than new. David Durochik/Sportpics.

{ FIGURE 3 }

This 1983 Mizuno World Win "Tsubota III" bears the name of the company's eminent glove designer, Yoshii Tsubota. He counts Ichiro Suzuki among his clients and fans. David Durochik/Sportpics.

Tightening the Laces in Any Glove

———

Here's something every major leaguer knows that you probably don't: you can rejuvenate a glove by tightening the laces. Craig Biggio has his tightened three or four times a year, whenever the glove begins to feel flimsy. If yours is so sloppy you're considering buying a new one, tighten the laces first. Chances are you'll be overjoyed to find you now have a glove that's firm but nicely broken in and fits your hand perfectly.

There's a recommended order in which to tighten laces, basically from the palm out.

* First tighten the palm lace (figure 2, item 1), which runs from the base of the pinkie down to the hinge and over to the base of the thumb. This lace snakes between the inside and the outside of the glove, and it's the toughest to handle.

  You'll need a tool—try a small pair of needle-nose pliers (figure 1, item 4) held closed. Pinch the lace between your thumb and the closed plier nose and pull it through, back and forth. If worst comes to worst, you can open the pliers, pinch the lace, and pull it, but this often disfigures the lace. An excellent tool instead of pliers is a brass lacing needle, available from The Leather

Factory in Fort Worth, Texas (leatherfactory.com). The four-inch version (figure 1, item 9) is strong enough to create some torque and has a softly rounded tip. This is nice because occasionally, if you're not careful, the tool can slip off the lace. You don't want needle-nose pliers flying around.

You can tighten the palm lace two ways. You can start at one end and end at the other, but you might encounter trouble at the hinge, where layers of leather get pretty tight. So it's a better bet to start at the hinge and work outward in both directions, leaving the hinge itself alone. Either way, tighten this lace lightly, no more. Overtightening can make your glove too stiff or—worse—tear the thin leather lining inside the glove, especially if it's older.

* Tighten the heel lace that loops around the glove's perimeter from the pinkie to the thumb (figure 2, item 2)—again, no more than medium firm unless your glove's a rag and you want it rock hard.

* Tighten the three-loop laces that pierce the thumb and the pinkie (figure 2, item 3), tight if you like those digits curled inward. Some repair people do these laces last, especially for outfielders,

who tend to prefer longer, straighter fingers and thumb.

* Tighten the web lace. On most gloves the web lace runs straight through the tunnel at the top of the web. It's inside there— it's not the corkscrew lace (figure 2, item 5) that's a continuation of the fingertip laces and emerges at the tip of the thumb. Start tightening the web lace where it emerges at the top front of the thumb and index finger (figure 2, item 9). Pull this lace forward here to take up some slack, and you're on your way. Now work your way downward. Depending on the glove, you may only have to work the perimeter of the web, as with a Rawlings Basket Web. On others, like most "open" webs or "H" webs, you'll zigzag from the perimeter to the middle and out again a few times before you reach the bottom. On some gloves you might encounter a knot halfway down the web on the back. A new segment of lace begins immediately below this. If you have a good mental picture or a pencil sketch of the web before you start, you should have no problems. Most webs tie at the bottom in back (figure 3, item 4), where they meet the pocket of the glove. Sometimes there's some crisscrossing of the two laces inside the glove here, but if you've come this far, you can figure it out. Don't bother to try to tighten the lace that corkscrews along the top of the web—it's not usually worth the effort.

* Tighten the crisscross fingertip laces (figure 2, item 6). On most gloves, the corkscrew lace from the top of the web continues on to the top of the fingertips, thus running from thumb-tip to pinkie-tip. Start where it emerges from the web and work toward the pinkie, pulling and tightening as you go. In some gloves, like older Wilson A2000s, the finger lace starts and ends at the pinkie, never reaching the web (a brilliant idea). It makes a U-turn at the index finger. Regardless of the glove, the clever X pattern that all fielders' gloves use today will begin to seem logical too, as you work at it. Tighten this as firmly as you want, but not to the point that you pinch or gather the leather.

Tying tip: where two laces are tied together, glovemakers use a good old-fashioned square knot, which is less inclined to come loose. Starting with a lace in each hand, bring the left lace in front of the right,

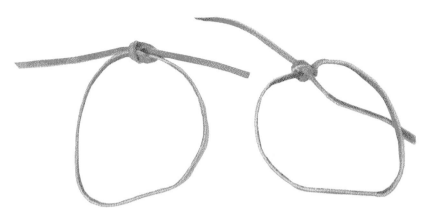

[Tying tip]

Use a square knot (left) to cinch laces tight wherever two come together, such as on the thumb and pinkie and behind the web. Practice looping one around the other just right to avoid getting a less-than-secure "granny knot" (right). Photo by Noah Liberman.

loop it over, and pull it back through underneath (see photo above). Now reverse this, bringing the right lace in front of the left, looping it over, and pulling it back through underneath. If it doesn't, you've done a "granny knot" (above right), and it's likely to come loose.

Replacing the Laces in Any Glove

—

Sometimes tightening laces isn't enough. If a lace has broken, you'll need to replace it, and if other laces look frayed or thin from years of stretching, consider replacing all of them (figure 1, item 11). Should you do this yourself? Not if you don't like a manual challenge and certainly not if you have a big game tomorrow, because the first attempt often yields bizarre results. There are hundreds of glove-repair

people who can relace a glove for $40 or so. Some are profiled in Chapter 8. Or call a good mom-and-pop sporting goods store near you and see if they can recommend someone with experience. Shoe-repair people are hit-and-miss with glove lacing. Some are excellent relacers and have all the right materials. Others use cheap, leftover leather cut from belts or whatnot or don't follow the original lacing patterns.

If you relish the challenge of relacing your own glove, here are some tips:

* Lace for gloves comes in ¼-inch and ³⁄₁₆-inch widths, the latter in two thicknesses, the thinner being for the palm lace. You can get laces from these folks: The Glove Doctor, who sells a handsome dark brown lace in addition to the classic tan and black (thesportsdoctor.com, 609-252-9340); Glovesmith, whose laces

are the best, some say (glovesmith.com and 888-331-4100); and Triple C Leather, whose laces sometimes have a slightly orange tint (800-927-1212). Most sporting goods stores sell brown laces in bubble packs, but they're not as good as those offered by the outlets above. Don't buy from a shoe repairer unless he or she assures you that the laces are specifically for gloves. Try to use laces of the same size and thickness as the manufacturer did, but in a pinch you can do the whole glove with ³⁄₁₆-inch laces and not suffer.

* Use either a brass lacing needle with a tapped-out end (figure 1, items 8 and 9) or a long-handled lacing needle (figure 1, item 7) with an eyelet at the end. The latter is available in lacing kits sold at most big sporting goods stores. The brass needle is a bit easier to weave in and out, and once you've attached the lace to it, you don't have to mess with it until the lace is finished. It is available in two sizes from The Leather Factory (leatherfactory.com). But many glove-repair people swear by the long-handled needle, which you insert, attach the lace to, then pull through, repeating the process until the lace is done.

* Before starting, satisfy yourself that you understand the glove's lacing patterns. Take a picture of the glove if you have to, or draw a diagram. You'd be surprised how easy it is to forget some important detail and find yourself lost. Note a few important things:

* where each end of the heel lace rests, on the front or back side of the glove (figure 2, item 7)
* where the palm lace emerges from the back of the glove at each end (figure 3, item 8)—there are several possible places, such as from a web hole or a heel hole or even a hole all its own
* Webs are the trickiest part of a glove, by far. Consider unlacing and relacing the web simultaneously: loosen the knots and start pulling one lace out, replacing it with the new lace as you go. You can't replace the web lace on most fielders' gloves without undoing the corkscrew lace that continues on to become the X-laces of the fingertips. Undo the corkscrew lace, or take the entire thing out, if you plan to replace it. Relace the web, pulling the new lace straight through at the top to start and then working down both sides simultaneously. When the web is done, you can relace the corkscrew around the new web lace, or you can replace it entirely, starting at the thumb-tip, on to the corkscrew, and then to the X-pattern at the fingertips.
* As you replace laces, err on the side of too loose. Once you've laced a glove and learned its pattern, it's a snap to tighten laces after a few games when you know exactly what you want. But if you make them too tight to start, it takes forever for them to break in again, and you could tear some leather before that.

Don't let the name fool you: the Sandalady, Fran Fleet, left footwear behind 30 years ago to start repairing baseball gloves. Photo by Sterba Co.

CHAPTER 8

Strange but True:
Glove-Repair People

*"I get gloves that have electrician's tape and gaffer's tape or those electrical-tie things.
I have one today with shoestring. I love it when people tell me, 'It's an emergency
repair, the kid has a game at 3:00,' and can I do it now, and they have 17 knots
in the glove, and I say, 'It's not* really *an emergency—
it's only an emergency because you don't have room for another knot!'"*

—*Fran Fleet, the "Sandalady," baseball glove repairer*

There might be a hundred people in the United States who don't just slip on a baseball glove. They slip it on, slip it off, then snip all the rawhide laces with a side-cutter and yank them out. Then they whisk all the crud out of the fingers and palm and scrub the glove, inside and out, with Murphy's Oil Soap or Glove Loogie's "postseason" formula or even lacquer thinner. Then they run eight or nine feet of brand-new, alum-tanned rawhide lace through it and apply mink oil or Vaseline or Glovoleum or Lexol or, if they're old-fashioned, neat's-foot oil.

A few of these folks, the ones with powerful sewing machines in their basements, will cut out the rotted, mouse-eaten lining and replace it. Or they'll patch tears between the fingers or even sew the thumb back on after the dog's had his way with a beloved Rawlings Reggie Jackson.

None of them can get rid of mildew, however. Mildew's your fault, and they can't undo it.

If you don't know these people, you should, because you'll need one someday. If your glove's got a busted lace or a creeping tear, you need one right now. If it's old and floppy and you're about to retire it, don't. Fork over 40 bucks and have one of them relace the whole thing. It'll spring back to life, pleasantly firm and shapely, just like after you broke it in. Can you think of a better way to spend $40?

These are glove repairers, and they go by such names as the Glove Doctor, the Glove Master, the Glove M.D., the Gloveman, and the Mitt Mender. One of them goes by the Sandalady, even though she graduated from smelly footwear 30 years ago. "There was a crossover time when I did both sandals and gloves," says Fran Fleet. "It's just too complicated to change names."

These people have skills. It takes Kenny Gand, the Mitt Mender of downstate Rochester, Illinois, no more than half an hour to relace a glove, with a minimum of six different pieces of toughened cowhide. These include the short, vital loops that keep the thumb and pinkie rigid and flat.

And the two long laces that run like lifelines over a glove's palm, except that they're not exactly like lifelines: you can replace these and turn back the clock, feel like your best days as a fielder are still ahead. There's the lace that crisscrosses the fingertips. If you want to, tighten just this one on your own glove and add another season to its life. And finally there's the lacing for the web. You and I might stare at it for half an hour and still not know where it starts and stops, but the Mitt Mender and the Glove Master and the Sandalady know the patterns by heart.

They're self-taught. They learned through trial and error, error at first. Dick Stump, the Glove Master, bought himself a $15.95 Mickey Mantle MM3 in 1959, one of Rawlings' top gloves and one of the best gloves ever made. But Stump's broke immediately. "I was a third baseman, and the first line drive tore right through the web. Now if you're a kid, I was 15 or 16, you're looking at this brand-new glove and wondering, 'How the hell do I get this web back?'" He didn't wonder long. Stump bought some rawhide lace at a shoe-repair shop, bent the end of a coat hanger around it, and hit the hanger with a hammer to secure it. "I laced it right through." Then he got fancy. He noticed all the black gloves in newspaper

*Dick Stump ruined his brand-new Mickey Mantle MM3 44 years ago trying to dye it black.
He's restored 25,000 gloves since then.* Photo by Noah Liberman.

pictures and decided he wanted his black too. "I dyed it and ruined the living hell out of it. I didn't realize the gloves were all dark brown and it was just the newsprint that made them look black."

Ten years later Stump found Fiebing's Leather Dye, and he's used it on many of the 150 gloves that hang from the wall of his tidy Hobart, Indiana, shop. He thinks he's fixed 25,000 gloves in the past 40 years. He put a black web in Ozzie Guillen's glove 15 years ago, when the rage among Latin infielders was multicolored gloves. He'd come a long way from his first dye job.

This is just one small corner of Dick Stump's meticulous Indiana workshop. Photo by Noah Liberman.

Once watching Dave Kingman's glove being repaired, Richie Ashburn said, "They should have called a welder."

Fixing gloves is what Stump did when he got home from his job as a steel cutter at Inland Steel, and it's the focus of his retirement now.

John Golomb is self-taught like the others, but he had an advantage. His father owned the Everlast Company, which started as an all-purpose local sporting goods store in the Bowery 90 years ago and became the top name in boxing a generation later. Golomb had access to leather and sewing machines, and he invented the thumbless boxing glove in the early eighties. Years before, his own Rawlings Playmaker—the classic glove with three fingers that a generation of kids grew up with—fell apart, and he decided to just make himself a new one. "I took it apart and made a copy of it. I didn't have the right leather, though. Leather to make training bags with, thinner and stiffer. It didn't really turn out right."

Now it does. Golomb, the Glove Doctor, makes about 250 gloves a year in Belle Mead, New Jersey. Half of them are full-sized modern styles and half are sturdy, playable replicas of earlier models, from Babe Ruth's white Draper & Maynard "Lucky Dog" glove to seventies-style Wilson A2000s or eighties-style Rawlings XPG6s. He designs his own gloves, too, like a monstrous thing with a thumb on each end for players who like to keep their options open. "I sell about 10 of these a year, to ambidextrous pitchers," he says. If there's a flaw in this model it's that it's too heavy. But there's a compact little infielder's glove he makes that incorporates the innovative lacing patterns from Wilson and Rawlings, the angular shape of MacGregor's best seventies models, and strong, supple leather from tanneries in Mexico. It'll set you back $350, and it'll make you happier than the four bills you plunked down yesterday to take your buddies golfing.

But most of the work these people do isn't so high-concept. Tom Alexander is the Glove M.D., and his lacing jobs are catalog-perfect, consistent, and straight, not too tight and not too loose. Starting each January, he'll do hundreds of gloves for colleges around his Sacramento, California, shop, and in February he'll handle the high schools with a one- to two-day turnaround. Through the summer he'll hit tournaments of all kinds, shoring up 2,500 gloves before he settles in for the colder weather and a steady mail-in business.

It pays the bills. Alexander is a divorced father of two. He says he pulls in between $30,000 and $50,000 a year, an honest living made one rawhide lace at a time.

It sounds about the same for Fleet, who lives in Cotati, California, just north of San Francisco. "I'm not living in the big house and driving the big car, but I'm paying my bills, and that's what I'd do if I was doing anything else," she says.

There are other benefits. Occasionally the glove repairers have a brush with fame. Golomb has done work for lots of major leaguers in New York, including a few he can't name because the work involved sewing a Rawlings logo on a Wilson glove or a Mizuno on a Louisville Slugger. It's a fact that some major leaguers will follow the money to a richer endorsement deal with a new company but won't give up the old glove. A new logo satisfies everyone, because that's what shows up on television or the cover of *Sports Illustrated*. Golomb did this for a modern-day Yankees pitcher who later threw a perfect game, but he won't say which pitcher. Take a guess. You've got a 50-50 chance of being right.

Golomb came up big for Wade Boggs once, too. The superstitious third baseman couldn't part with his Rawlings, which was in tatters from a decade's use. Boggs wouldn't send him the glove, either, for fear it would get lost. Golomb met him at Yankee Stadium and promised to restore the glove. "I'm driving down the turnpike that night and I don't have the slightest idea what to do with this glove, because Boggs doesn't want me to change the way it looks with patches and stuff. And then it hit me." He made a special new lining and sewed it in as unobtrusively as possible. Now he has a picture of Boggs in his workshop inscribed, "To the Sports Doctor, from one glove guy to another."

If Fleet's done famous gloves, she's not telling. "I don't follow the game. I fix gloves, and I'm totally indiscriminate about who I fix for," she says. "Now if a famous ballplayer from Willie Mays' era came in, I'd probably pee my pants."

That's about as revealing as Fleet gets. She comes across stubborn and proud. She won't divulge the recipe for her own glove potion, called Glove Stuff, and she gets testy

Babe Ruth visited the Draper & Maynard glove plant with his Red Sox teammates early in his career and tried his hand at sewing. "I can hit 'em better than I can make 'em," he muttered.

when a reporter gets technical with his questions. "I could write my own book," she snaps. And she's irritable with the glove companies. Nokona's leathers are too soft, she says. Wilson's earlier A2000s had thumb loops that didn't tighten far enough. The "ridiculous" double-D snugger on the back of Rawlings' ubiquitous Fastback models "only wads the leather up."

She sounds like Stump. "The guy who invented the Basket Web for Rawlings,"— renowned designer Rollie Latina, actually, with nearly 30 patents to his name—"didn't know what he was doing. Every time you catch with it it stretches, and there's no way to tighten it." Rawlings' Davey Lopes model XPG 16? "Another idiot designed this. There's no strap to hold the web at the bottom. Do you know how many of these I've had come in torn?" (It's no wonder Rawlings won't take Stump's calls anymore.) "And the companies will never learn you don't put plastic inserts into the thumb of a baseball glove."

Talk to a few glove repairers, and you start to see a pattern of stiffness and independence. Maybe it's because they're self-taught and they have that feeling of singular accomplishment. Alexander started fixing gloves as a young man, and it was how he kept himself in beer in the navy. "I'd get off a plane at some base, and guys would be standing there with broken baseball gloves and cases of beer. I don't think I paid for a beer for two years back then." Or maybe they're self-taught because they're stubborn. He worked for Apple Computer in the eighties, until he was laid off. Apple said glove repair was interfering with his work. He replied, "You're kind of right, you just have it backwards. This day job is interfering with my outside interests."

Lee Chilton, the Gloveman of Fremont, California, is from the same mold. He had a huge glove-repair business in the eighties, was profiled by *Sports Illustrated,* and says he was interviewed by anchorman Chet Huntley. He's crusty, and he switches direction like Andruw Jones. "There's no such thing as an expert," he says. "People who have done things for a long time, society labels them experts, but it's just a way society has coined to fool people. I'm like Leonardo DaVinci, man. People catch me at the freeways, hospitals, doctor's offices, and they remember my face. Nobody in this country has gotten up in glove repair the way I have."

Golomb might be just a little touched too, in the manner of artists. Ask him if the glove leather today compares to that of your youth, and he says, "I haven't seen anything that compares." You ask for an explanation and soon you realize he meant the pre–Industrial Revolution leather tanned in upstate New York. But he's on a roll and you don't force him back on the subject. "The water," he says, "the materials that go into it. . . ." and you ask if water really does affect leather. He says yes, and you ask how, and he says only that Philly cheesesteak sandwiches taste "awful" in Los Angeles. That's when you realize he's prone to free-associate and think in analogies. "What makes a Stradavarius?" he demands. "I rest my case." There's a pause. "The kind of wood he used . . . they think he found it alongside a certain river. It was aging there a while, something like that. Something about the paint. Ever seen the movie *The Red Violin?*"

Where the **Pros Turn**

Many major leaguers do their own fix-it work, especially for some reason catchers, like Detroit's Brandon Inge. You can find him in front of his locker with one of his small Wilson 2403 mitts and a long, red-handled lacing needle, yanking new rawhide through the web. "I break laces all the time, so I'm always restringing them," he says. "I love gloves, always have. And I love fixing my glove, because it relaxes me and it makes me feel like it's mine."

But most players let someone else do the work, like an equipment manager or a coach. Tom Probst does it for the California Angels; he is one of many athletic trainers who learned the glove art in the minor leagues, at the same time they were doctoring pulled hamstrings and carrying equipment and booking motels and even pulling tarp—earning their keep.

And there's Bob Patterson, known as the Glove Doctor (and not to be confused with the Belle Mead, New Jersey, Glove Doctor John Golomb; apparently there can be more than one Glove Doctor). The fine relief pitcher retired in 1998, after a 13-year career with five teams. He fixed hundreds of different gloves in his day. Glove companies kept him in tools and new laces. And he helped Easton develop Doctor Glove, its lanolin-based conditioner.

His reputation was solid. "My glove has missed a third of an inning in the past eight years," shortstop Gary DiSarcina said a few years ago. "I popped a string and Bob fixed it in two minutes." In fact, Patterson was the only person DiSarcina allowed work on his glove. Opposing players would ask Patterson to fix their gloves, too, but he'd turn them down. Except one time. "In Kansas City, [dexterous second base-man and former teammate] Chico Lind

Bob Patterson was a better-than-average reliever and a world-class glove repairman. Tony Inzerillo/Sportpics.

came up to me before a game and was begging me to work on his glove. He'd worn a hole right into it, another case of a guy being so attached to one glove. So I was in the bullpen, stitching some new leather over the padding, and there was a ball up the middle and he booted it, right into center field. I looked at him, because he never booted that ball. It was his gamer I was working on. He looked back at me and threw down the glove he was using. Here I was, never supposed to work on the opponent's glove, and I helped us out."

An array of "gamers"—
game-used gloves that
belonged to
(counterclockwise
from top left):
Alex Rodriguez,
Joe Hutchinson,
Tony Gwynn,
Mike Piazza,
Pedro Martinez,
Kirk Gibson,
Willie Mays,
and Joe Medwick.

Sold in Mastronet auctions.

Copyright © MastroNet Inc.

CHAPTER 9

Weird Science:
What Major Leaguers Want in a Glove

"I tease [Barry] Larkin and tell him if he had a decent glove he'd never make an error.
His glove is stiff and the fingers go out in funny directions.
But gloves are like bats; what feels good to one guy doesn't to another."

—former Cincinnati Reds coach Ron Oester

There's a science to how major leaguers choose a glove, but it's not a very rigorous one. Every major leaguer sounds convincing when he explains his preferences. But when you listen to several players, you start to hear contradictory theorems. You try to reconcile them, but finally you understand players wear the glove that looks right and feels . . . *right*. Don't you do the same?

Take fingers, for example. For a few years now, many major league infielders have been letting their glove's fingertips spread wide. The glove breaks in and the fingertip laces stretch, but the players don't bother to tighten them. Some old-guard infielders do this— Walt Weiss was one—but mostly it's the younger ones, like Cesar Izturis, Mark Bellhorn, and Ron Belliard. Second baseman Belliard's fingers are so splayed, the glove looks like it's been hit by a cartoon steamroller. And many players who don't let the fingers spread wide still like to bend the thumb and pinkie out. Why, after 125 years of glove evolution, did players hit upon this supposed improvement? You never get a complete answer, just hunches mostly. "I'm not sure…no, I'm not sure why players do that," says third baseman Eric Chavez, who does it. "The glove doesn't come that way. I just do it myself." Ricky Gutierrez is nearly as vague. "I don't stick my hand all the way in a glove, I leave it [partway] out. So that's probably why it's wide like that. When I break my glove in, I always turn the [pinkie] end of it out."

Do they want more surface area, maybe? "Yeah, that's part of it," Chavez says, as if he just thought of that. "Hmmm, yeah," Gutierrez says.

Surface area makes sense, but so does Travis Fryman's explanation for having done the opposite—keeping the fingertips tight. He says it helped the fingers lie flat on the ground for low hops. But even Fryman

In vogue: the Cubs' Mark Bellhorn and Sammy Sosa show the current preferences in gloves. Bellhorn's small infielder's model is loose at the fingertips and Sosa's long outfielder's model is festooned with embroidery, including the Dominican flag. Style notwithstanding, Bellhorn and Sosa knocked heads on this play; the ball dropped and Sosa missed several games with a strained back. Al Podgorski, *Chicago Sun-Times*.

curved the thumb and pinkie out, and Jeff Huson, for one, never understood why: "Why would you want your fingers bent out so that the ball could possibly hit the tips of the fingers and not
go directly into the glove?" he asks.

Ozzie Guillen did it the old way. He cinched the fingertips tight and curved them in a little, as did earlier generations of infielders, players like Ozzie Smith and Joe Morgan and Mike Schmidt—the way anyone over the age of 30 did as a kid, too. "I always liked it tight, so when the ball hit this part of my glove, it's not open and it stayed closed," Guillen says. "And when people want to make the play but [the ball] hits out here [on the fingertips], it's harder." But how does he explain his former teammate Weiss' preference for splay? "He catches the ball a different way, he tries to catch everything in the palm." And Ozzie didn't? "Aaaahhh, I don't think I got the good hands like he does," Guillen laughs. He's talking about what major leaguers call "hands guys," infielders who field the ball in the palm, as Jackie Robinson and Pee Wee Reese did 50 years ago because their smaller gloves made it imperative, and as Vizquel and Robbie Alomar do today because they're virtuosos.

So you can ask a bunch of infielders about the fingertips of their gloves and get a lot of answers that sound logical, but finally they boil down to hunches and preferences backed by a bit of impromptu mechanical theory.

The rest of the glove science is this way, too. There's some hard science involved— like why middle infielders' gloves usually are wider than third basemen's, and why third basemen's are almost always wider than outfielders'. But there's just as much hunch-following, fashion-trending, and copycatting going on.

Take color. When Manny Trillo had the back of his tan glove dyed black in the late seventies, he set off a fashion trend that evolves to this day. First Latino infielders followed his lead. Aurelio Rodriguez broke in rookie teammate Tim Flannery's glove in 1980 by first coloring it with magic marker and shoe polish, and Flannery loved the glove for six years. But now you can find factory-made multicolored gloves at every position, although glovemakers and players suggest that Latino and black players still lead the league in fashion. Sammy Sosa's long Rawlings is light blue and orangish-red and festooned with the flag of his native Dominican Republic and the names of his

Manny Trillo is said to be
the first modern player to
appear with a multicolored
glove, dyeing the back of
his tan glove black in the late
seventies. Tony Gwynn
did the same to his 1986
gamer (shown on pg. 90).
Nowadays, manufacturers
will give players almost any
combination they want.

Tony Inzerillo/Sportpics.

children. Tony Gwynn's glove had contrasting lightning bolts on the backs of the fingers. Barry Larkin's gloves have had various combinations of black, red, and gray. Raul Mondesi's have been scarlet and navy.

Still, there is a little science to glove color. Omar Vizquel won't use a black Rawlings because he says they're stiffer than the brown ones. All of Huson's Rawlings were black, and when he tried a brown one once, "it just didn't look right or feel right, for some reason." Jim Hughes, Rawlings' vice president of professional baseball, acknowledges that dying a glove black puts a little more "tension" in the leather, makes it a bit less supple, which is why catchers tend to favor tan gloves. Overall, black gloves outnumber brown ones slightly in the majors today, although the gap has closed in recent years. You'll find the black-glove majority greater among outfielders, who follow fashion whims more than any other position, while infielders, like catchers, favor brown gloves for the suppleness.

As for copycatting, look at two pitchers, Greg Maddux and Pedro Martinez. They're the style leaders among white and black/Latino pitchers respectively—because they're among the best pitchers, period. Several years ago, when Wilson outfitted Maddux with a glove featuring its Conform wrist adjuster, a smaller opening in the back, and the Pro-Sleeve finger protectors, the glove became the most popular among Wilson's pitchers in two quick years. "Every pitcher either uses it or takes a good look at it," said Wilson's top glove marketer, Jim Hackett, a few years ago. Curt Schilling wears a similar glove, but probably for what he considers good, scientific reasons. He's the pitcher who has every pitch he's ever thrown on digital video in his laptop computer, after all. But other pitchers followed Maddux because he's Maddux. Same with Martinez. Pedro wears a small two-tone Rawlings, black with red or orange laces— except when finicky umpires make him exchange it; pitchers aren't supposed to wear multicolored gloves. The glove has a "modified Trap-Eze" web (a single middle bar secured with laces on each side that shimmy back and forth). It's an infielder's glove, really, but Martinez wears it, and so do a few dozen more pitchers in the Rawlings stable—and many more in other companies' who just want a little of Pedro's magic.

Lanky and style-conscious (his sideburns are cutting edge), closer Kerry Ligtenberg uses a Rawlings much like Martinez's, and it looks comically small on

Greg Maddux (far left) uses the biggest legal glove available, and his fielding shows the results. Pedro Martinez (middle) wears an infielder's-size glove and, until 2002, got away with illegal contrasting webbing. Kerry Ligtenberg (right figure at right) follows Pedro's example, with a glove that's strikingly small against his tall frame. Maddux and Martinez photos by David Durochik/Sportpics; Ligtenberg photo by AP/Wide World photos.

Joe Morgan's (second from right) gloves were so small, teammate Dave Concepción (second from left) used Morgan's extras in fielding drills to improve his hands.

From the Rucker Archive.

his hand. "I feel more comfortable with a small glove," he says. "I don't really know why. I just feel more comfortable not digging around for the ball when I'm getting ready to pitch." In fact, pitchers throughout the majors are using smaller gloves these days. A handful of old white males—Maddux, Randy Johnson, Roger Clemens—use longer gloves similar to the big, floppy things Dennis Eckersley and Rollie Fingers wore a generation or two ago. But they're the exception. Reliever Lorenzo Barcelo, at 6'4" and 230 pounds, wears an infielder-size glove, even though his middle finger is four and a half inches long. Chicago White Sox trainer Joe Nossek said the only major leaguer he's seen with bigger hands is Michael Jordan. "Sometimes it *is* a little too tight," Barcelo told a reporter. Satisfy the vanity before anything else, apparently.

Brett Butler's defensive weapons: a quick jump, good speed, and a glove the size of a bushel basket.

Ron Vesely/Sportpics.

Occasionally players use a fielder's glove at first base. Stan Musial did until Rawlings invented the six-finger Trap-Eze that he could wear at any position. Jose Offerman played first base with a fielder's glove in 2000, and Ken Caminiti did the same in 2001, when he couldn't get used to the longer first baseman's mitt. Finally he had a short mitt made and nicknamed it "the Taco." The Major League Baseball rule book states a player can wear a fielder's glove at any position, including first, but mitts only at first and catcher.

Baseball gloves were smaller than a man's hand when Cincinnati catcher Doug Allison wore the first glove recorded in a major league game, in 1870. His glove had half-fingers and no padding. From there gloves grew fairly steadily for 120 years. Willie Mays made "the Catch" in 1954 with a Harvey Haddix pitcher's model, a little over 11 inches long. Mickey Mantle's last Rawlings was around 12 inches long. About a decade ago, Brett Butler, Luis Polonia, and Ruben Sierra—two short guys and a butcher—sported 14-inch bushel baskets. (For a glove's official length, you measure from the bottom of the heel to the tip of the longest finger with the measuring tape flat against the palm of the glove all the way. Twelve inches is the maximum allowable length for gloves, but umpires will always give an inch.)

Hoyt Wilhelm said Gus Triandos was the best at catching his knuckleball, that he didn't even need an oversized mitt. Replied Triandos: "I think he was kidding about me being the best catcher for his knuckleball. At first I didn't need the big mitt, but later I did. The more you caught him, the worse you got."

Orioles skipper Paul Richards had a huge mitt made in 1959 so his catchers could handle Hoyt Wilhelm's fluttery pitches. Joe Ginsburg, pictured here, was wearing the glove when he let three Wilhelm pitches by him for passed balls in a single inning, tying the record his teammate Gus Triandos had set a week before. Could this account for his ironic smile? From the Rucker Archive.

Outfielders' gloves have settled down to 12¾ inches for the vast majority, while infielders' gloves have undergone some shrinkage in the past five years.

If you follow the trends in infielders' gloves through the decades, you see the gloves growing steadily through 10 inches in Pee Wee Reese's day to around 12 inches in Brooks Robinson's. Robinson wore the same glove as his outfielders—literally, because he often traded them two gloves for one—at a time when third basemen and outfielders wore virtually the same glove, a 12- or 12½-incher. Today only Robin Ventura and Vinny Castilla and maybe a couple of other oldsters wear outfield-size gloves at third. This is because when Joe Morgan lopped two inches off a Luis Aparicio model in the late sixties and sported a ten-inch stub, he started a gradual trend on the infield. No one after Morgan used a glove as small as his—the ever-thinking second baseman wanted the extreme of agility and quick release, like his predecessor Bill Mazeroski—but infielders liked Morgan's theory, and today most second basemen have gloves 11 inches long or shorter. Most third basemen's gloves are less than 12 inches, and shortstops' are between 11 and 11½ inches. "I'd say infielders' gloves have lost a half inch over the past five years," says Rawlings' Hughes.

But what about first basemen and catchers, who catch more balls than anyone? Their mitts tended to lead all positions in innovation, like Hank Greenberg's huge fishnet web in the forties and the rudimentary hinges in catchers' mitts around the same time, many years before fielders' gloves adopted the breakthrough feature. But now, mitts change less from year to year than gloves do.

First basemen's mitts grew steadily for almost a century, to a peak of around 13 inches in the seventies, and today only a handful of first-sackers wear one smaller, by a half-inch or so. The rule forbids first baseman's mitts longer than 12 inches, but who's measuring? Catchers' mitts never have been much for extremes in size either, except for knuckleball catchers' mitts, which reached the size of Thanksgiving platters in the mid-sixties before the current rules came into effect. When hinges became universal by the early seventies as catchers went one-handed, the mitts began to change shape, gradually becoming less round, more oval and clawlike, almost like thickly padded first basemen's mitts. Bob Boone used a strikingly small mitt in the eighties, around

13 inches long. The rules prohibit a catcher's mitt longer than 15 ½ inches long, and catchers don't exceed this. Some, such as Jason Kendall and converted shortstop Brandon Inge, use one an inch shorter.

Maybe first basemen and catchers don't need to experiment much any more, having helped pioneer gloves almost 130 years ago. Maybe they can't afford to, or don't need to, because their job is more about just catching hard throws than about catching myriad throws—and hits and hops—and then making a quick release. Catchers are considered the most finicky players about their mitts, but not so much about performance features, as these are fairly standard. They're finicky about how the mitts feel, and you can't blame them any more than you can blame Allison and his sore hands. "Charles Johnson, for a guy who's won so many Gold Gloves, is extremely picky about his gloves. From one day to the next, I don't think even he knows what he likes," says Steve Cohen, Rawlings' East Coast glove representative. For their part, pitchers are superstitious (see Chapter 10), and sometimes flashy, but not obsessive about a glove's performance features. "Just give me the biggest legal glove and I'll learn how to use it," multiple Gold Glover Greg Maddux says. It's infielders who fuss about size.

And it's outfielders who are particular about shape. With few exceptions, outfielders like a long, narrow glove. Bad caroms off lush outfield grass cause them no nightmares, but not reaching a liner in the gap or losing ESPN time when they can't pull a home run back over the fence does. It's possible that every major league outfielder wears a "closed back" glove today, with the single hole for the index finger to escape. The finger dividers in this kind of glove extend down farther toward the hand, because there's no opening at the back of the hand. This feature allows outfielders to wear the glove out on their fingertips and gain an extra inch or so of reach. Yet 15 years ago you could find plenty of outfielders who weren't ready to accept closed-back gloves. Otis Nixon says they made him claustrophobic. "I couldn't have the closed one; it felt too tight. I tried to use one and I just couldn't." Today, an exception to the preference for narrowness is Ichiro Suzuki, whose glove is softer and wider than most outfielders', in the Japanese style. His glovemaker winks and says it's because Ichiro likes to catch balls behind his back. Considering Ichiro's cachet, do you foresee the next glove trend?

But if you really want trends, look to second, short, and third, where players tinker like mechanics. In the small-pocket days of Jackie Robinson, gloves were relatively wide and shallow, naturally. They grew deeper through the fifties and sixties, but then Morgan, with Mazeroski's example, revived the shallow pocket. Today, there's a wide range, from Bret Boone's shallow one to Alex Rodriguez's deep one, but some earlier stars say they're too deep overall. "Some of the kids I work with today don't really know how to break in a glove to be a middle infielder. The pocket's too small and too deep," says Johnny Goryl, a Cleveland Indians coach whose playing career ended in 1964.

One of the reasons pockets may seem deeper is that gloves' heels have shrunk steadily for 60 years, leaving pockets proportionately larger. Next time you're in a sports store, compare gloves' heels to the one on your favorite old glove—and compare yours to the Charlie Brown–style glove your father used. Players at all positions have always wanted as little heel as possible, and so for decades they shaved the heel padding as part of the break-in process. "You know, it never entered into anyone's mind to ask for smaller heels," Goryl said. "They just figured we all wanted to break in a glove our own way." Today glovemakers make surgery unnecessary, although

companies do have reputations about their heels. Mizuno's are the narrowest—too narrow for Fryman, who preferred the slightly wider Zett. Rawlings has the reputation for the widest, one reason Mark Grudzielanek sticks with a midsized Wilson despite overtures from Rawlings.

At the same time, Mizuno has a reputation for the softest leather—in stark contrast to the harder gloves it has always made for the Japanese market—and Zett's and Rawlings' are considered hard.

For all the concern for design, where the glove meets the palm you find guys going with their gut. How can you sort through the following contradictions? Joe Morgan started wearing a batting glove under his glove later in his career. "It made my hand fit tighter in my glove," he says. Walt Weiss never did. "It makes the fielding glove feel too loose," he told one writer. Ozzie Smith never wore an extra glove. They covered up "the most sensitive part of your hand," the spot between the index and middle finger, he says. Kevin Elster wears a batting glove precisely to cover that spot up. "It affects my fielding when I think I'm going to feel pain," he says. Guillen might be strangest of all. In his rookie year a trainer gave him a knit glove to wear underneath on an icy April day. It felt so good, he wore that style for 16 years, no matter how hot the weather.

But inside the glove is where you do find one or two apparently scientific truths. Many pitchers and outfielders put their pinkie and ring finger in the pinkie slot and locate each of the other two fingers one slot over to the left. David Wells does it, Bernie Williams does it, and so does Brady Anderson. Pitchers simply say they aren't interested in getting a bone bruise fielding throws from the catcher. Outfielders say it promotes a snap action. "I don't want to have to squeeze the glove around the ball, I just want it to hit and have the glove close on its own," Anderson says. You won't find an infielder doing this, for the opposite reason pitchers *do* do it: they need to feel the ball in the palm. And the best of them don't close the glove around the ball anyway. Smith essentially paddled the ball from his

left hand to his right, and Vizquel does the same. Mazeroski would tip slow rollers off his pinkie or heel. Frank White, who played a fine second base for Kansas City from 1973 to 1990, told an interviewer late in his career that Mazeroski had the quickest hands he'd ever seen. When the interviewer reminded him that Maz had retired before White broke in, White said, "No, I'm talking about his hands *right now*. I've seen him fooling around with a ball. He has the quickest hands I've ever seen."

But I digress. Maybe there's no better proof that the glove reflects science *and* psyche than the fact that as players mature—and get better—they often start using larger gloves. Young ballplayers are like all young people, their self-image and ego intertwined. So a tiny glove stands for skill and confidence. A teammate jokes that Ligtenberg's glove is like "a college infield-

Paul Dickson's The New Dickson Baseball Dictionary credits Ken Harrelson in 1964 with the first regular-season use of a batting glove (it was actually a golf glove) but notes that Bobby Thomson was using golf gloves 15 years earlier in spring training. Others have noted that Mickey Mantle was wearing one in *Home Run Derby*, a TV program filmed in the winter of 1959–1960.

er's." Apparently college ballplayers have the most bravado. Casey Wise, a journeyman infielder whose last game was in 1960, recalls his Pacific Coast League coach urging him into a bigger glove. Robby Thompson made the switch himself halfway through his career, around 1990, and Ray Durham did the same a few years ago, at manager Jerry Manuel's urging. Said current infielder Eric Hinske in his second year in the majors: "I was at 11½ inches, but I'm gravitating toward a larger glove as the years go by. I'm more confident I can get to more balls to my right and left." Here at least is a case where science and psyche seem to mesh.

So that's the science, more or less, of major leaguers and their gloves. It's not a hard science but one softened by subjectivity, by feel, and by fashion. Maybe there's one eternal truth. Says longtime Reds infielder and coach Ron Oester, "I'm a righty, and if I put my hand in a lefty's glove, they all feel good."

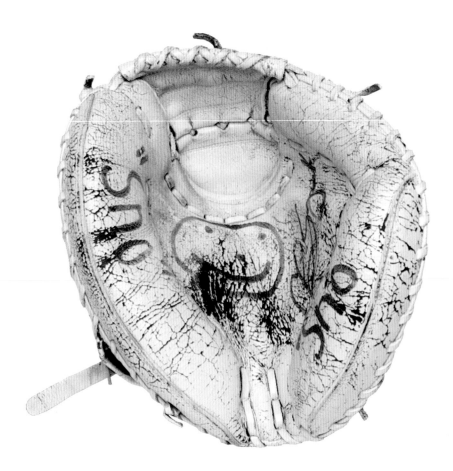

Rookies are often sent out to catch the ceremonial first pitch, a sign of their lowly status.
So when he was with the Chicago White Sox, young infielder Chris Snopek took the joke a step further,
whitewashing this mitt and festooning it with silly art. Teammate Davey Martinez went Snopek one better,
autographing the mitt on the back in ballpoint pen. Dave Durochik/Sportpics.

CHAPTER 10

Name It, Sweat It, Bronze It, Lose It:
The Lighter Side of Major Leaguers and Their Gloves

"It was bronzed while he was using it."

*—former Pirates manager Danny Murtaugh to a fan who'd joked he saw
Dick "Dr. Strangeglove" Stuart's glove bronzed in the Hall of Fame*

Except for maybe his protective cup, a major leaguer spends more time with his glove than with anything else he owns. A love develops, and as in all love affairs, strange, funny, and even sad things happen. Here are some details.

Precious Metals

What is it about Yankees pitchers and bronzed gloves? There are several stories about Yankees having their gloves immortalized, and when you're talking Whitey Ford, Bobby Shantz, and Sparky Lyle, you're talking three pitchers who deserve the fame.

Ford kept two six-finger Spaldings from his playing days, the one he wore to start his 33-inning World Series shutout streak and the one he was wearing when it ended. The latter's not in playing condition, though, because Ford used it to make the mold for a bronze lamp in its likeness. The metalsmith had to push a pole up through the middle finger first. A regretful Ford told a collector at a card show a while ago, "Yogi [Berra] talked me into it."

Shantz seems a little regretful about one of his gloves, too. "It was beat, I mean really beat," he told a glove collector. "I had it with me after I retired, when a guy came up to me one day and asked to have it to bronze it. He did, and I couldn't believe it came out so great. It was beautiful, and here was a glove that had the lining gone and the strings busted, and it just looked great. I wanted to get it back, and the guy wouldn't sell it or anything. He still has it on display at his shop."

No regrets for Lyle, though. Lyle livened up a dull Yankees team when he joined it for the 1972 season. For one thing, he had the team play "Pomp and Circumstance" when he came to the mound. His 35 saves led the American League, so he decided he wanted his glove bronzed. He'd had it since his minor league days. "I thought bronzing a dying art," said Marty Appel, the longtime Yankees public relations boss. "But we finally found a place, and they put it on a stand for him."

The Gold Glove trophy isn't real gold—it's a real leather glove painted gold. Omar Vizquel pulled one of his apart and took infield practice with it! Courtesy of Rawlings Sporting Goods.

On the Indians, shortstop Omar Vizquel also has no regrets and apparently little ego about his Gold Gloves. Rawlings glove representative Steve Cohen presented Vizquel with one of his many Gold Gloves one day before a game. "He took it off the stand and started using it to take ground balls for a couple minutes," Cohen said. "It's a real glove, just gold-colored. Everybody just laughed. That's Omar. But no one ever saw anyone pull the trophy apart like that."

Lost (or Stolen) Art

When you're famous and your glove gets lost, you usually don't get it back. Amos Otis had two gloves in 22 years, stretching from high school in 1963 to his retirement from the majors in 1984. The first glove was stolen in 1972 shortly after he showed the old thing on national television. Reggie Jackson's glove was stolen at the 1993 All-Star Game. He'd used it for 17 years, until

he retired in 1987. Barry Bonds and Marquis Grissom, among others, have had gamers filched too.

But sometimes the glove comes back. Bill Mazeroski lost track of a glove after one season, but teammate Roberto Clemente showed up with it the next spring. Mazeroski would use a glove until it was a wreck, and Clemente claimed none of the kids he knew in Nicaragua would take the glove off his hands that winter.

And country music star Garth Brooks was reminded he wasn't quite major league material when it came to gloves, either. In the Mets camp one spring for his annual baseball fantasy, he left his glove on the field and it disappeared. He asked Rawlings glove rep Cohen for a new one, and they spent some time pawing through Cohen's van to find one that matched. "I'm sitting there," says Cohen, "and he's describing it to me, and I turn around and there's a garbage can. I say, 'Does it look like this glove?' and

Robby Richardson, Bobby's oldest son, rode off to a game with one of his dad's patent leather Gold Gloves (in the days before statues were awarded) before his dad caught him.

he says, 'Yeah, like that—wait a minute, that is my glove!' It didn't have his name on it, so it got thrown in the trash."

Name on the Glove

—

By the early nineties, many players were having names—theirs or others'—embroidered on the thumbs of their gloves. Glove historians think Pete Rose was the first, with his blockbuster endorsement deal with Mizuno in the mid-eighties. Today roughly 75 percent of all major leaguers have something embroidered there, usually their name in cursive. But they get creative, too. Ray Durham has had "Sugar Ray" on his. Pedro Martinez has the names of his four kids. Andruw Jones has had the flag of his home Curaçao on his, Rafael Furcal the Dominican flag, and Orlando Hernandez the Cuban flag. Joe McEwing apparently was so fond of Rawlings' glove rep Steve Cohen that he put "Stevie C 47" on his—47 being McEwing's number. Rawlings now has an official SC 47 model glove, too.

The Glovesmith company sells gloves to minor leaguers at cost and one day got a request by fax for a glove with an unprintable two-word expletive on it. "We just ignored it," says owner Mike Seawel, "and four weeks later we get a call from a player asking for his glove, and we can't find the order, and we ask him to describe it. He's hemming and hawing, and finally we realized it was the obscene glove. We didn't make him that glove."

Before glovemakers did the work for them, players inscribed their gloves. Many inked their numbers on the back, where thumb meets strap. There's something majestic about the big "7" found on some of Mickey Mantle's earlier gamers. (Kids used to ink a 7 on their Mickey Mantle models too.) It's fascinating to think that Mantle needed to identify his glove so he wouldn't lose it—just like everyone else—yet in 1999 one such glove went for $239,000 at auction. Some of his later game gloves have "MICK" on them instead. By then, Mantle knew he was an icon and not just a number.

Tony Pena's first Gold Glove trophy was stolen the day after he got it.

As a youngster in 1956, Mickey Mantle inked his number on the strap of his glove, like everyone else. Later in his career, he graduated to "Mick." Nowadays, players put Mantle to shame where individuality is concerned. Courtesy of Rawlings Sporting Goods.

Jokes and admonitions have been common, too. Fine third baseman Graig Nettles had "E-5" on some of his gloves, and the waggish Robin Ventura had the same on a glove that he posed with on the cover of *Sports Illustrated* a few years ago. Now that took confidence!

Amos Otis' longtime gamer had perhaps the most poignant inscription of all. As he was being eased out of center field by the Royals at the end of his career, he wrote "LEFT FIELD" and "RIGHT FIELD" on the fingers. When he was benched, an anonymous teammate wrote "PLAYS NO MORE" on a remaining finger.

What's the Name of Your Glove?

When ego and spare time come together, you get players giving their gloves nicknames. Just a few that have gone beyond the dugout and into the public domain are George Scott's "Black Beauty," Aurelio Rodriguez's the "Black Hand," Ted Simmons' the "Big Trapper" (which he said had been "trapperfied"), Mel Hall's "Lucille" (which he kept in a state of disrepair) and Dusty Baker's "Sure-Catch." Paul Russo, a journeyman minor league utilityman in the nineties, called the glove he used

at third base "the Machine." He said he made only seven errors in seven seasons with it, but he never made the majors.

One of the cleverest names was Red Murff's "the Moneymaker," punning on the "Playmaker" and "Haymaker" models made by Rawlings and Nokona respectively in the fifties. Murff was the scout who discovered Nolan Ryan, and before that he had a stellar minor league career, going 146–95 with a 2.96 ERA. It's inconceivable that such a pitcher would have only four major league decisions today, as Murff did. Murff was a fine fielder, and he wrote that the glove kept him in Cokes, as he always won the low-stakes pepper games with his teammates. Tired of losing, one day in 1957 his mates held a funeral march down the first-base line in Wichita and buried the Moneymaker somewhere near the warning track. Years later Murff returned and tried to find the glove, with the help of an anthropologist and a metal detector. All they found were beer tabs. "Maybe Murff buried his beer there," one wag said.

The Long-Lost Practical Joke

It's popular to say baseball isn't what it once was, that money and fame have made

Yankees second baseman Billy Martin turns two while an opponent's glove observes from shallow center field. Until 1954 players left their gloves on the field when their team went in to bat. Naturally, practical jokes ensued. From the Rucker Archive.

the major leagues a less happy place. Well, here's proof. It's impossible to get a current major leaguer to recall a practical joke involving a glove. "Go ahead and put the shower shoes in the freezer, but don't touch the glove," says Reed Johnson, Toronto Blue Jays center fielder.

It didn't used to be that way. In decades past, practical jokes with gloves abounded,

even though everything about a glove seemed more precious.

Things had to be looser if Joe Morgan was the butt of a joke. Morgan and Jon Miller make for a charming broadcast team on ESPN these days, but Miller supplies most of the levity; Morgan's a famous stickler about the game. In his playing days, he made a scientific study of the glove—size, shape, how to break it in—and he'd use a glove for five years or more. So this story is telling: "I had an incident with the Reds when I went 81 games before making an error. That day in San Diego I'd made three—me and [the Padres'] Tito Fuentes too—by the third inning. After the game [Pete] Rose and [Johnny] Bench took a big old garbage can and taped my glove to it and said, 'Take this out and get rid of it!' I'd been mad and it kind of relieved me."

But many of the best stories come from even looser days, like the years before 1954, when major league players still left their gloves on the field between innings. Maybe because their gloves spent half the game in the public domain, players didn't grow quite so possessive of them. This explains why Eddie Stanky could hide Bill Rigney's glove under the second-base bag and once kicked Bobby Thomson's glove to the wall several innings in a row to show contempt for the rookie. Johnny Pesky, a serious hearts

player, once found the dreaded queen of hearts in his glove, according to the 1990 "Glove Story," one of the most enjoyable *Sports Illustrated* pieces in memory. In the late thirties, Billy Rogell put a dead sparrow in Oscar Melillo's glove after Melillo had nabbed him with the hidden-ball trick. Two decades later, several Washington Senators tricked catcher Clint Courtney by unlacing his mitt and putting Limburger cheese inside. Teammate Russ Kemmerer said the umpire had a tough time leaning in to call balls and strikes that day.

Perhaps the excitable Phil Rizzuto was the victim of most tricks. He found a dead rat in his glove one time and a dead sparrow another, the story has it. And Eddie Joost says he got Rizzuto with a rubber alligator. Joost says he warned the second-base umpire, Bill McGowan, and the two watched as Rizzuto, hysterical, tossed the rubber gator 30 feet in the air and screamed, "There's a big animal in there and it bit me! Look!"

When the Detroit Tigers walked out to protest a suspension of their star, Ty Cobb, a team of local amateurs was assembled to play the A's. Tiger ace George Mullin handed over his uniform and locker to his replacement, an Aloysius Travers, and said, "Kid, you can steal anything but don't take the glove."

Superstitious? Naturally

Something happened in 2001 that shows how obsessive many players are about their gloves. Seattle's Bret Boone was signing autographs before a game and mistakenly tossed his own glove to a fan instead of the one he'd signed. Boone was frantic, and the word went out. The fan was found, and Boone gave him an autographed bat in exchange for the glove. "This is a lot better deal," said the fan, Daryl Carr, a Microsoft employee. "I'll take this any day. [Boone] said it was a glove he was breaking in for next year, and that he couldn't live without it."

Maybe Carr had never owned and loved a glove, because he didn't seem to understand that he'd just traded a one-of-a-kind reflection of Boone's body and soul for a piece of ash just like dozens of others in the storage room. But he was happy, and so was Boone, who'd lived through a glove-man's nightmare. (And Boone is a glove-man; his peers admire how quickly he gets rid of the ball on the pivot and say he'd have a Gold Glove if not for Robbie Alomar's stranglehold in the American League.)

Players love and depend on their gloves so much, many get anxious. Fear of loss. Fear of sharing. Fear of the glove itself, if there's no other explanation for sudden failure. Anxiety is at the root of all the stories that follow.

Lend a glove to a buddy? "NEVER," barks All-Star first baseman Jim Thome. "I hate it when somebody touches my glove. You can grab my bats, but not my glove." Almost every major leaguer feels this way. For a few it's a concrete matter. Longtime utility infielder Jeff Huson chastised a groundskeeper for putting on his glove one day. "He didn't understand this is how we make our livings, and it has to conform to your hand, and if somebody goes and jams their big old fat fingers in there, the glove changes forever."

But for most it's a matter of superstition or karma or cooties. Defense is reaction, not assertion, so there's always the fear the ball will start to play you, cosmically speaking. So don't upset the cosmos by letting someone else's hand in. "I'd never share my glove. And never let a pitcher touch your glove," says Eric Hinske, the Blue Jays' promising young third baseman.

Or maybe just let people touch it in certain situations. "I would allow people to pick it up," says Ozzie Smith, "unless a guy was in an awful slump. 'Get your hand off that! Don't bring me that problem!'" Joe Morgan never let his gamer touch another, but he'd let Dave Concepción practice with one of his spares. Morgan's tiny 10-inch gloves sharpened the skillful Concepción's hands—and why not let another future Hall of Famer borrow your glove?

Major league infielder-turned-coach Tony Taylor used to sit on the bench with his glove on, just to keep it safe. It irritated his new teammates in Detroit, he says. Huson was one of many players who set the glove down thumb-up, a symbolic way of keeping control of it when they bat. If he found it overturned, he righted it immediately. But perhaps the most fragile psyche was Urban Shocker's. "If you got hold of his glove between innings, he was licked," twenties pitcher Eddie Rommel said in the book *Peanuts and Crackerjack*. "He used to lay it on the ground until the opposition coaches got in the habit of picking it up in passing. After that he carried it to a special spot on the bench."

You can hardly blame a player for being superstitious, given all the evidence that messing with glove karma is a bad idea. Otis Nixon had an errorless streak going until he switched gloves. He was camped under a fly, "then a raindrop came into my eye and [the ball] hit the glove and it dropped and gave me the error and broke the streak and that's why I had to stay with the same glove all the time," he says. That story is so absurd it has to mean something. Here's another: Doug Dascenzo was close to setting the record for errorless games in center field when the rock group Alabama visited Wrigley Field and took batting practice. Dascenzo became enthused. "Doug being the nice guy he is and not thinking too much," Ryne Sandberg recalls, "he autographed his game glove and gave it to the guys in the group, and went out that day and made his first error."

But for all the players who know—or have learned—to keep their gloves to themselves, there are still a few who say they don't care. Mark Grace once told a writer he'd lend a glove to a teammate in need, then handed the writer his gamer and sauntered off for a cigarette and a card game, saying, "Just toss it on the chair when you're done." Grace himself benefited from David Segui's generosity after Grace's equipment got lost in 1995 on the way to Montreal. Segui and Grace shared one glove, leaving it on the field between innings, sandlot style. "I got some good ESPN time for that," Grace told MLB.com.

Derek Jeter said he'd be happy to lend his glove to a teammate. But that was a few days before one swiped his gamer—like this one—from his locker and sold it to a memorabilia dealer. Sold in a Mastronet auction.

Copyright © MastroNet Inc.

Derek Jeter, too, said he'd lend a glove to a teammate. "I'm not superstitious," he said a few days before Ruben Rivera swiped his glove from his locker, sold it to a memorabilia dealer, and got cut from the Yankees.

For all the fear of loss, sometimes there arises a fear of keeping a glove, and a player flees to a new one. Usually this player is a pitcher. Pitchers are the least attached to their gloves. They seem to want something that looks good and balances with their body. The slight Greg Maddux wears the biggest glove of any pitcher, while his closer, Kerry Ligtenberg, wears a tiny open-webbed glove. Pitchers are the quickest to jettison a glove when they want a fresh start on things. Closer Gregg Olson told a teammate, "The old glove was getting hit. I had to make an adjustment." No less a rationalist than Maddux has made the move. Phillies pitcher Randy Wolf recalls, "I was pitching against Maddux, and in the first inning he gives up four runs. He's wearing a brown glove. The next inning it's a black glove. He gives up no runs for the next seven innings." He got the win, too.

Throwing Caution to the Wind

—

There's an announcement before every major league game that fans are not to enter the field of play. But they defy it all the time in every way, as when 12-year-old Jeffrey Maier reached onto the field of play to turn a fly out into a crucial home run for the New York Yankees in the 1996 playoffs. There was the time Chicago Cubs fans dumped beer on Lenny Dykstra as he settled under a deep fly, and the time they littered the outfield with Randy Myers posters after Myers had blown a save. Recently—and here's a novel idea—a fan apparently poisoned a swath of Wrigley Field ivy during an interleague game with the White Sox. Yet players are surprisingly compliant when fans act up, except maybe for Rickey Henderson, who regularly chewed out Yankees fans who turned singles—in Rickey's mind—into ground-rule doubles by snagging balls as they rolled down Yankee Stadium's left-field foul line.

Rarely it's the player who scales the wall, as when the Los Angeles Dodgers, furious over a stolen hat, went after some Chicago Cubs fans a few years ago. Aren't you surprised that doesn't happen more often? More charmingly, usually it's the glove that goes up and over, not the player. Just like Bret Boone, Andre Dawson temporarily lost one a few years ago, when he tossed it to a fan instead of tossing back the fan's glove, which he was autographing before the last game he played at Wrigley Field. Boone and Dawson both got their gloves back.

Hall of Famer Billy Williams used to toss his glove to a fan after the final out of every season. "The first kid I'd see, I'd throw it to him," Williams told the *San Mateo Times*. "It got to be a habit. But the gloves weren't that special to me. It was a vital part of my equipment, but my main stress was in hitting the ball." There have been other on-purpose throws. Infielder Russ Johnson had a rough start to his rookie season in 1997 and tossed his glove into the Astrodome seats after committing an error that led to two unearned runs. He had a lighter brown one broken in and ready to go. "If it's as good as I hope it's going to be, it'll last a lot longer than that one," he told a reporter. You get the feeling that once a player has Glove number 2 broken in, he can start to lose confidence in Glove number 1.

Sometimes a player's aim fails him, as it did Roberto Clemente in Milwaukee's

County Stadium one day in 1959. The glove soared over the dugout and into the hands of 11-year-old Scott Bear, who took off like a shot. Later that night, under parental guidance, Bear called Clemente at his hotel. "No, you keep it," Clemente said, and hung up. Today, a kid who lucks into a future Hall of Famer's gamer sells it on eBay for a thousand bucks or more. Four decades ago, Bear took it to school the next day and played with it for two years until one of the laces broke. He sold it recently, a Herb Score Personal Model.

So there are purposeful tosses and accidental tosses, and then there are disputed tosses. Dave Campbell was a weak-hitting infielder before he became a heavy-hitter in ESPN's baseball coverage. Do you believe the ballplayer/journalist when he tells this story? "It was spring training in Scottsdale, 1971 or '72, and at that time it was the absolute worst field to play on, every hop was a bad hop. One day Ron Santo was just having a horrible day. He had a couple errors, and a couple of bad hops hit him in the throat and hit him in the shoulder, and some fan was just heckling the crap out of him behind third base. He came in after one inning and the fan was on him and he just took the glove and threw it up there and said, 'If you can do any better, you get your butt out here!' I don't know if he ever got the glove back."

Santo denies everything. He says he once lost a glove the way Boone and Dawson did, giving his gamer to a fan while signing autographs, but Campbell's recollection? "That story's not true," Santo says. "I would not do that."

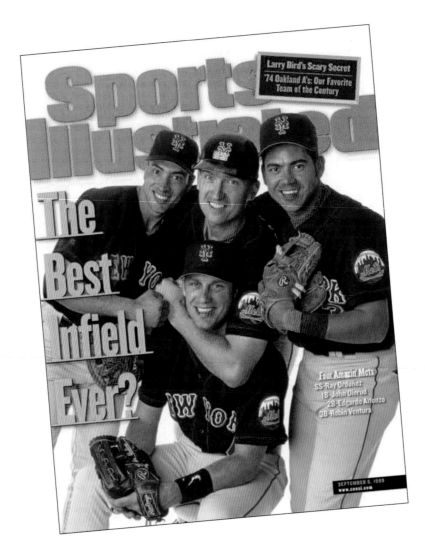

Rawlings won the brand war on this Sports Illustrated cover with four logos on two gloves
(belonging to Robin Ventura and Edgardo Alfonzo). The exposure might have been worth a million dollars.
Sharper eyes are needed to discern a pair of Wilson logos on Rey Ordoñez's glove, tucked
behind the headline. Sharp eyes might also note that Ordoñez's first name was misspelled on this cover.
The mistake was not caught until many subscribers had been mailed the incorrect version. V. J. Lovero/Sports Illustrated.

CHAPTER 11

Lawyers, Gloves, and Money:
The Endorsement Game

"Stan Musical"

—The stamped endorsement on a Rawlings Stan Musial personal model glove from 1949, the kind Musial himself wore. It's not known if it was a mistake or a joke.

Endorsements are as natural to pro sports as groin pulls.

In 2002, golfer Tiger Woods had endorsements with roughly a dozen companies, worth $55 million a year. That was 10 times what he made actually playing golf the year before.

Sometimes the deals overshadow the athlete. Consider that tennis "star" Anna Kournikova made $20 million for endorsements in 2002 while ranked around 40th in the world and having never won a WTA singles tournament.

In baseball, players have been endorsing gloves since the 19th century.

Endorsements are predicated on simple, subjective logic, the logic of association. *Tiger Woods is a great golfer. Tiger endorses American Express. American Express must be a good credit card.* Actually, it can be even more subjective. A sign at an Indy Racing League event a few years ago read, "I STOPPED USING TIDE WHEN ROBBIE LOST HIS RIDE." That fan was going to use whatever laundry detergent gave his favorite driver a deal. The fan spent with his heart, because his T-shirts were going to come out fairly clean regardless.

*The white Draper &
Maynard G41 was a
hot seller in the mid-
twenties, and Babe Ruth
was baseball's first great
endorser.*

From the Rucker Archive.

So it's no surprise that baseball glove endorsements began, though modestly, almost as soon as major leaguers were wearing gloves.

Cincinnati catcher Doug Allison is the first pro known to have worn a glove, back in 1870, and sporting goods catalogs were offering gloves to the public by 1872. Albert Spalding, a great player and a great sporting goods entrepreneur, was the first first baseman not to be ridiculed for wearing a glove, in 1877. Fans loved Albert, and when they didn't hoot at his glove, he offered it the next year in his catalog. He called it the "Spalding Model," and it's the first time on record that a player's celebrity was used to sell a baseball glove.

Spalding was also the name of his company, so the endorsement wasn't quite as personal as it is on the Derek Jeter model Rawlings your daughter or son wears today. But no one who bought the Spalding Model (a half-fingered buckskin glove with no padding) failed to think of Albert.

From there developed one of the most entertaining facets of the baseball business. It grew slowly at first. Endorsements weren't widespread until after World War I, and around the turn of the century the player's name often didn't appear on the little glove itself but on the hangtag that accompanied it. But when Babe Ruth became baseball's first true nationwide star and his name appeared on Draper & Maynard's top-of-the-line G41 model—in a swank, white sueded leather—it touched off an endorsement push that never has stopped.

The endorsement biz has also never stopped evolving. In Ruth's time, most glove companies weren't nationwide, and most stars weren't nationwide either. So a company would sign players from teams in its region. And there were so many small companies by the thirties, nearly half the major leagues were appearing on a glove. Try hard enough and you can collect endorsed gloves for the entire starting lineup of the pennant-winning 1934 Detroit Tigers, as collector Don Millington has done, or 23 players from the 1940 Cincinnati Reds, as collector Joe Phillips has. Even as late as 1963, 42 different players' names appeared on at least one Rawlings glove. All but the four top-priced $43.50 "Professional Models" of the company's 55 gloves that year had someone's signature or block-letter name on them.

In the 2003 Rawlings catalog there are 127 gloves and only six player endorsers: megastars Derek Jeter, Alex Rodriguez,

Pocket Art

A ballplayer's handsome cursive signature is what we usually see on the palm of an endorsed glove today, but in the past, glovemakers were more flamboyant. They stamped everything into the glove but the kitchen sink—as far as we know.

Collectors have turned up a Wilson with "Little Luke McCoy" on it, from *The Real McCoys* TV show of the fifties. Popeye's cartoon likeness was on a thirties glove. Norm Zauchin, a fifties first baseman, had an autographed glove with "PLAYBOY" in the pocket. It's not known whether that refers to Zauchin or the magazine, which was founded in 1953.

Glove expert Joe Phillips, who publishes *The Glove Collector* newsletter, has compiled a list of surprising nicknames, like "Little Sprout" on a Lloyd Waner glove, or "Chappy" on a Ben Chapman. But it's believed Joe Medwick never allowed "Ducky" on any of his.

Mistakes were made. There's a "Ruddy York," a "Harvey Kuen," a "Bobby Schamz," and a Japanese-made "Mike Franagan." Nokona got Tony York's name right but accidentally stamped it twice into a glove now owned by a collector. Elmer Riddle appeared on so many military-issue gloves that it's thought his might be the most prolific endorsement ever. But a "UAS" designation on one has experts confused. Should it have read "USA"?

Shantz was disrespected in another way. He was the Gold Glove pitcher in the years after the award was begun in 1957, but Rawlings put Harvey Haddix's name on its top glove, not Shantz's. This shows that endorsements are based on fame, not necessarily on glovemanship.

And this is why it's not uncommon for famous noncatchers to have endorsed catcher's mitts—stars like Cy Young, Rogers Hornsby, Ty Cobb, Honus

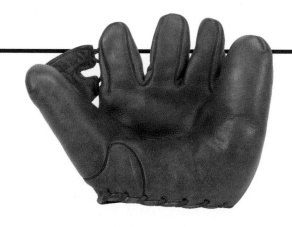

Martín Dihigo played Hall of Fame–caliber baseball
in the outfield, the infield, and as a pitcher during
a long career in the Negro Leagues and in Latin
America. But since the American major leagues
were off limits to him, so was a glove contract with
an American company. His endorsed Hercules
Company models, made in Mexico, are worth
thousands of dollars to collectors today.

Sold in a Mastronet auction. Copyright © MastroNet Inc.

Wagner, and Lou Gehrig. Eighty years ago, Chicago White Sox catcher Ray Schalk had a "Schalk Special" fielder's glove with hometown sporting goods company Wilson.

Roy McMillan had his name on a kid's glove for Wilson, but he hated the thought of it.

Regrettably, there are no American-made gloves endorsed by Negro League players, and very few Monte Irvin gloves and no Luke Easter or Sam Jethroe gloves have shown up, although the Denkert company made many Hank Thompson gloves and Caprico and Dubow made Jackie Robinson gloves.

Collectors wonder why it appears Jimmy Collins, Chief Bender, Burleigh Grimes, and Hoyt Wilhelm never had endorsed gloves. And they wonder just who are Johnny Mack, Larry Steinbeck, Bill Schroeder, and Hank McDonald, who appear on Hutch gloves from the sixties and seventies. No major or minor league records exist for any of them. Many such mystery names have appeared on gloves through the decades.

In fact, here's how easy it was to get your name on a glove. Tom Casagrande, a Phillies farmhand in the early fifties, never made it to the majors and later became partner in a sporting goods store. He told a Stall & Dean salesman he'd buy 100 gloves if the company would put his name on them. Stall & Dean did.

So is *your* name on a glove?

Ken Griffey Jr., Mike Piazza, and Mark McGwire, and mere All-Star Jorge Posada, who gives the company an American League catcher and one who appeals to young Yankees fans. Only 25 gloves bear one of these endorsements; 23 of the endorsed gloves are for young players, and the most expensive of these is a midpriced $73 Ken Griffey Jr. model.

America is more sophisticated now, apparently. Television, radio, and the Internet have made every star a national star. And there are almost no small, regional glove companies. The business is dominated by behemoths like Rawlings and Mizuno and Wilson, and they can cover a lot of territory with a handful of endorsers. A young fan in Milwaukee can easily find a Derek Jeter mitt; if he wants a José Hernandez, he'd better go to Miller Park and get José to sign it himself.

The endorsement business has always been a messy affair. Literally. Names were misspelled on gloves. Sonnett put the name of fine Yankees pitcher Bobby Shantz on its K4F model. Trouble was, they spelled his name "Schamz" on the glove. A Japanese company had a "Mike Franagan" model in the seventies. Poor Mike Flanagan.

It's been a legal mess too. For a few decades, laws allowed any company to put "DiMaggio Model" or "DiMaggio Style" on its gloves as long as it was in block letters. This is not allowed today; a player controls almost all uses of his name. The legal wheels began to turn with a landmark 1935 federal case between two bat companies, the upstart Hanna Manufacturing Co. and the behemoth Hillerich & Bradsby Co. Lou Gehrig made rambling testimony on behalf of H&B, explaining that he felt he'd given H&B the right to use his name to sell bats and Hanna only the right to put his name on bats intended for his personal use. Today legal scholars say the case helped affirm that fame is a "property" that can be used for monetary gain and thus deserves certain protections. Thanks to Gehrig and H&B, ballplayers are richer today. So are the Beatles.

In the days before every player had an agent—which is to say a lawyer—endorsements were up for grabs. Chico Carrasquel, who gave fans in the fifties a foretaste of the dancerlike style of current Latin shortstops, signed any glove contract put in front of him over the course of several years. He didn't know he couldn't grant the same right to more than one company. Other players did the same thing, and finally in 1956 the National Sporting Goods Association brokered a growing

They meant Shantz, not Schamz: the Sonnet glove company blew it on this model, intended to capitalize on fine Yankees pitcher Bobby Shantz.

David Durochik/Sportpics.

Shortstop Chico Carrasquel welcomed glove endorsement deals with open arms—until he realized he was supposed to sign only one. From the Rucker Archive.

dispute among all companies by forcing them to prove they had the first endorsement contract a player had signed. The small Nokona brand had Carrasquel's first deal, but Wilson Sporting Goods—then becoming a national power—refused to stop using Chico's signature on gloves. So the Texas-based Nokona found a local named Billy G. Martin and signed him to a glove deal, to steal the thunder of Wilson and its promising young endorser, the Yankees' Billy Martin.

Despite laws governing contracts and endorsements, there are gray areas even today. Companies have always known that some of "their" players aren't actually wearing their gloves. Robin Roberts, Richie Ashburn, and Willie Mays were MacGregor endorsers who used Rawlings in games. Mays made "the Catch" with a Rawlings HH—the Harvey Haddix model dozens of major leaguers were wearing then.

In pretelevision days, this kind of thing went on casually. With the advent of TV, players had to be more careful. "I used this old MacGregor for five years, and the whole time I had a Wilson contract," Toby Harrah told MLB.com a few years ago. "I would mark out the brand name. I really liked that glove." Today a player has his equipment manager cut off the offending logo and sew on the logo of the company he signed with. This company is satisfied, because it's the logo that matters—it's what shows up on *Baseball Tonight* or, better still, the cover of *Sports Illustrated*. (A one-page ad in *Sports Illustrated* runs about $250,000. When Robin Ventura and Edgardo Alfonzo posed with their Mets infield mates on the front cover of a 1999 issue wearing their gloves, with a total of four Rawlings logos clearly visible, it was worth several times that in exposure. Ventura and Alfonzo themselves made only a tiny fraction of that from Rawlings that year.) At the same time, the company

Lefty Gomez became a Wilson glove adviser in 1947. On his application, he gave the following reason for leaving his previous employment: "Couldn't get anyone out."

Rawlings wooed Nomar Garciaparra until he agreed to wear the company's glove. Soon he was headlining the company's web homepage. Courtesy of Rawlings Sporting Goods.

supplying the contraband glove is betting the player will jump ship once his contract is up. And jumping ship happens all the time. Roger Clemens has won Cy Young Awards in three different companies' gloves.

In every major league locker room you'll see lots of newspaper beat writers in bad clothing. You'll also see glove-company representatives in slightly better clothing. Every big company employs a few reps, and these folks hang out near lockers and ply key players with promises to build them the perfect glove. Steve Cohen is Rawlings' East Coast representative, and he keeps the company's stable of top shortstops happy, among them Derek Jeter, Alex Rodriguez, and Omar Vizquel. He spent much of 2001 wooing Nomar Garciaparra. Finally Nomar, Nomar's wife, and Cohen met over dinner. A few days later, Cohen got a call from Nomar. Nomar had agreed to jump ship from SSK to Rawlings. "I want to be known as the Derek Jeter of my profession," Cohen says.

What's in it for the player besides the right glove? For a very select few, like Ken Griffey Jr., a deal worth about $100,000 a year. It's small potatoes compared to what the shoe companies pay NBA stars, but baseball gloves are only a $170 million busi-ness at retail each year, while basketball shoes gross $2 billion. Rawlings might sell 500,000 Griffey gloves, but Adidas will sell many times that in Kobe Bryant shoes. In fact, shoes help explain why Nike got into baseball gloves in 2000—not to grab a share of the puny glove market, but to get its "swoosh" logos on still more TV sets and sports pages. So it can sell more of every-thing with the swoosh on it. Last year, retailers bought $9.9 million worth of stuff with the swoosh on it.

Almost every major leaguer has a glove contract, as do most top minor league prospects. Many get a few thousand dollars a year to sign, but some get no money at all. A few don't bother and just have gentle-man's agreements with companies. Believe it or not, Omar Vizquel is one of those. What the players get is two gloves a year made to their exact specifications—size, shape, color, embroidered names or flag on the thumb, whatever. Top players can get more gloves, within limits, as extra gloves come out of a glove rep's allotment. Jose Oquendo was playing several positions for the St. Louis Cardinals in the late eighties, and he asked Rawlings rep Bill Smith for a first-baseman's mitt, according to *Sports Illustrated*. "When I see it in the box score,

Wm Sullivan
Cincinnati Reds BB Club
Cincinnati, Ohio

State of Ohio
Hamilton County

I, the undersigned, hereby give and grant unto The P. Goldsmith Sons
Company, a Corporation of Ohio, for the sum of $5.00, receipt of
which is hereby acknowledged, the sole and exclusive right to the
use of my name, autograph, portrait, photograph, picture, initials,
or nickname, for trademark and advertising purposes in connection
with the manufacture or sale of Athletic Equipment and covenant
with the said The P. Goldsmith Sons Company for myself, my heirs and
assigns that said rights herein given shall be exclusive for their
use as against any and all parties, and I hereby consent to the re-
gistration thereof as a trademark (by said The P. Goldsmith Sons Co.).

I hereby advise that the Athletic Equipment bearing my name, or
other designations as above, was constructed in conformity with my
ideas and/or is being used by me.

I hereby warrant that I have not previously given my consent to any
agreement in any wise in conflict with the foregoing.

Signed in duplicate this **16th** day of ____**July**____, 193**5**, at
Cincinnati, Ohio

Gloves and/or baseman Mitts will be supplied for personal use
gratis during each playing season.

Hugo Goldsmith   *Bill Sullivan* (Seal)
    Witness
                                    1st Baseman

Billy Sullivan   *Billy Sullivan*

Billy Sullivan   *Billy Sullivan*

Billy Sullivan   *Billy Sullivan*

WP. Possessor — RL — small Heel

The Cincinnati-based Goldsmith glove company signed light-hitting first baseman Billy Sullivan to an endorsement contract midway through 1935, his only year with the Reds. It cost the company five dollars. In those days companies generally sold their wares regionally, so when Sullivan departed at season's end, the company saw no use for him in its 1936 catalogue. But a midpriced Sullivan catcher's mitt began to appear in 1939, the year after he had the best fielding percentage of all major league catchers while playing for the St. Louis Browns. (He'd converted to catcher in 1936.) Sullivan signed this contract seven times before the company had a signature good enough to use on a glove or mitt. The scribbles at the bottom of the contract indicate that Sullivan was requesting a Wally Pipp–model first baseman's mitt and a Red Lucas–model fielder's glove with a small heel. Eleven catchers besides Sullivan had endorsed mitts for Goldsmith in 1939. Why not, since contracts cost the company so little? Today, glove juggernaut Rawlings has just two catcher endorsers, Big Apple All-Stars Mike Piazza and Jorge Posada.

you can have a first baseman's mitt" was Smith's reply. Pretty soon Oquendo had his mitt.

Robin Ventura is flighty about gloves. He found one of his old ones in his kids' toy chest and wore it in a World Series game that night, because it felt good again. "Robin's great, though," Cohen says. "He knows he's finicky, so he'll order a dozen gloves but he'll insist on paying for them."

In general, the relations between players and glove companies have always had a quaintness that contrasts with the hammer-and-tongs relations between players and team management. In the early 20th century, players were overjoyed to be getting something for free. The fine third baseman Billy Werber had played four major league games when he wrote to the Draper & Maynard Company in 1931: "Am in receipt of your glove which arrived before your letter. I appreciate the gift as well as your promptness. It is satisfactory with me for

you to use my name in regard to using your glove." Young Billy meant "in exchange for," not "in regard to," but his point is clear: happy with the "gift," he's granting use of his name.

At midcentury, Nokona was signing minor leaguers to contracts almost by the teamful, to ensure it would have stars in the fold someday. Grateful, Carl Erskine and Billy Hunter both stuck with the company as accomplished major leaguers, even after Nokona offered to free them to find better deals. And Lonny Frey, the Reds' slick-fielding second baseman from the prewar championship teams, refused to sign any glove but a Rawlings in his retirement. "I didn't endorse [competitors'] gloves, so I can't sign them," he said. Today it's the gentleman's agreements for players like Omar Vizquel that charm us.

Relations between player and company aren't always friendly, though. A famous outfielder from the fifties and sixties told a

When he played for the Indians, Jeff Manto had 13 gloves, including two catcher's mitts, two first baseman's mitts, and a miniature infielder's glove to sharpen his skills. "The guys call me the Store, but the equipment man hates me," he told a reporter. (He took all 13 gloves on road trips.)

fan at a card show several years ago that his deal with Wilson for two gloves a year so irritated him that when he toured the factory one time, he took "everything that wasn't nailed down."

Rawlings planned to leave Graig Nettles' glove out of its catalog in 1979, cutting into Nettles' royalty chances. Nettles asked Frank Torre (Joe's brother, the former player and at the time a Rawlings glove rep) to reconsider, but Torre wouldn't, so Nettles complained to the Rawlings president, who gave Torre a hard time. Irked, Torre told Nettles he wouldn't have a contract the next year. Nettles got mad again and later that day played the game of his life, turning the 1978 World Series for the Yankees. The next year he wore a Louisville Slugger.

And in the era of lawyers, gloves, and money, there have been lawsuits. Bret Saberhagen signed a 10-year deal early in his career for two bats and two gloves a year. In 1986 he sued Rawlings, claiming the contract he signed when young and impressionable was costing him $50,000 a year. The suit was settled, and Saberhagen stayed with Rawlings, but companies have grown more wary since. They give "big" deals to a small handful of players and deals worth a few thousand dollars to the rest so they can catch a bit more air time or be able to claim half of all major leaguers as endorsers, as Rawlings does, or roughly 30 percent, as Wilson does.

Recreational participation in baseball and softball has dropped roughly 30 percent in the past decade, and no big company like Rawlings is turning a profit solely on gloves. Chances are, a major leaguer will never be significantly richer because of his glove deal. So much the better. Gloves are like family, and money does funny things to families.

Wolf Cries Maddux

The endorsement stories of Greg Maddux and the promising young left-hander Randy Wolf lace together entertainingly. Maddux is one of Wilson's top endorsers, wearing an oversized A2000 with the special finger sleeve he helped the company develop. But he was a Rawlings guy early in his career. He changed because Rawlings didn't show him enough love.

"Believe it or not, I had a hard time getting a bigger glove from them. But I was just a turd at the time. I didn't rate. I wasn't any good. I asked a few times, you know, but I was 1–5 and getting ready to be sent back to the minors, and I don't blame them." The day after Rawlings told Maddux no, a Wilson glove rep happened by Maddux's locker and made the deal of his career.

On the other hand, Wolf was a Wilson guy until a couple years ago. "I called and asked for the Greg Maddux glove, and they sent me one, but it was really small, and I called them up and said, 'Sorry, I don't want to inconvenience you, but this glove isn't right. I wanted the Greg Maddux.' The guy said, 'Well, Maddux has that specially made.' I go, 'OK, anyway, can I get that specially made?' And there was a pause, and he said, 'Greg Maddux has four Cy Youngs.'

Later that year a Rawlings glove rep was visiting the Phillies and Wolf told him he wanted to switch. "Two days later, it's amazing, I get two gloves in the mail from Rawlings and they look just like the A2000, with the finger coverings and the web." Apparently Rawlings had learned its lesson with Maddux.

Photo by Noah Liberman.

CHAPTER 12

Glove Collecting:
Stirring Passions for the Game

"The objects they cherish are inanimate substitutes for reassurance and care.
Perhaps even more telling, these objects prove, both to the collector and to the
world, that he or she is special and worthy of them."

—from Collecting: An Unruly Passion, *by Werner Muensterberger*

"A guy goes and spends $10,000 on a glove, and a lot of guys say, 'That guy has a lot of money
and no brains.' Well that's just bull[bleep]. If a guy has a lot of money, he can do what he
wants with it. If he wants to pay that much for a glove, let him pay it. Problem is,
it dries up the market, and us guys at the bottom of the market get [bleeped] off."

—a veteran glove collector

These statements—singly and together—sum up the hobby of glove collecting.

There's the part that stirs tender feelings as it brings a baseball fan closer, in a tangible
way, to the game he or she loves. You'll see this in the way people collect. Howard Singer of
Dundee, Illinois, had 95 different Nellie Fox–endorsed gloves at last count. He has a soft
spot for the second baseman who played 15 of his 19 seasons at Comiskey Park in Chicago,

an hour away from Dundee. There's left-handed Gordon Eaton, who collects south-paw gloves. (He sells them too; his sales motto: only lefties wear their gloves right.) Richard Macaluso, a catcher in his sandlot days, collects catchers' mitts and probably is the world's top authority on the evolution of the "pud." These collectors go about their hobby humbly: if they feel they're *special* and *worthy*, this is a pleasure they take quietly, for few others know of their efforts.

Maybe Barry Halper had a greater need to be special and worthy. The Newark, New Jersey, native was already a voracious collector as a boy and had 75 major league uniforms by the time he graduated from high school. As a minority owner of the Yankees he got to know just about every player worth knowing, and so his stunning collection of memorabilia grew to 80,000 pieces, including 30,000 baseball cards alone—and Ty Cobb's dentures.

He sold 2,500 pieces in a 1999 Sotheby's auction, which netted $21.5 million. Then, if not long before, Halper's virtues were proved to the world.

Glove collectors everywhere can take pride in the fact that a glove was the most expensive item auctioned by Sotheby's during those two days: Lou Gehrig's final first baseman's mitt, the one he tossed to clubhouse boy Pete Sheehy, saying, "Pete, I won't need this anymore." Penny Marshall, the actor and director, bought it for $387,500. The fourth most expensive item was a glove, too, a Mickey Mantle Personal Model Rawlings XPG3, worn in games and autographed by Mantle himself, which Sotheby's identified as being from 1960; collector and top Rawlings expert Denny

Glove collector and Rawlings history savant Denny Esken despaired of having Nolan Ryan sign a glove at an autograph show in Pittsburgh several years ago when he saw 250 people already lined up outside. But he bumped into Ryan in the eighth-floor elevator and introduced himself. Ryan stepped out of the hotel (no unofficial autographs were allowed on hotel grounds) and happily signed a glove for Esken there.

Esken felt it was no older than a 1966 model and informed the winning bidder—actor Billy Crystal—immediately after. But Crystal didn't care. It was worth $239,000 to him just to own a Mantle "gamer."

Esken, by the way, owns the glove Mantle wore to make a great catch in Game 5 of the 1956 World Series (the glove on the cover of this book). Recognize the game? It was Don Larsen's perfect game. Crystal's glove made no such catch, so Esken is sitting on a gold mine.

The big price tags are impressive, but consider this as well. Crystal paid more for Mantle's run-of-the-mill glove than another collector paid for Mantle's one-of-a-kind Triple Crown trophy from 1956. All in all, the Sotheby's results proved with big numbers what Singer and Eaton and Macaluso prove with small ones, that for a fan there is no object quite like a baseball glove for getting at the essence of the game and the player both.

Or for stirring up the pure competitive juices seen in the second epigraph at the top of this chapter. The glove-collecting hobby virtually didn't exist 15 years ago. Joe Phillips' first issue of *The Glove Collector* newsletter, in 1990, was a page long. In the third issue he had to explain the difference between a glove and a mitt. Today there can be hundreds of collectible gloves available on the Internet auction site eBay at one time. Several sports auction houses offer gloves in every season's auction, and routinely some fetch $10,000 or more.

And there's a flurry of activity feeding this marketplace. At the bottom are the folks who sell the contents of a loved one's attic to an antiques dealer or a flea-market

Minnesotan Jane Homme lost her good friend Tim Page, 36, after a fall in 1991. She had bought him a Nokona Carl Erskine replica glove for his upcoming birthday. So his family allowed her to lay the glove in his casket with a note inscribed on the palm and placed "closest to his heart," she told *The Glove Collector* newsletter.

vendor. They rarely get what the glove is worth. Glove collectors scour the flea markets and junk shops and antique stores and bargain for the gloves. If they buy a glove, they do it knowing they'll make at least $20 on it; if they're smart and the junk dealer is unschooled or indifferent, they can make thousands on it. A Babe Ruth "gamer" was bought for $95 in a Minnesota antiques mall last year. The buyer sold it for $25,000 to Dave Bushing, a top collector and consultant to several big auction houses. Bushing turned it around immediately, although he won't say what it fetched. "I got my 15 percent fee," he says, smiling. Bushing was a well-educated UPS driver in Texas when glove collecting first got going in the late eighties. Buying and selling became his full-time job in 1991. Now he says he pays the IRS six figures in taxes each year. He wears sweatshirts, cargo pants, Birkenstock sandals, a goatee, and a shaved head, and he works out of the basement of his Northbrook, Illinois, home.

The hobby has been deeply affected by eBay. It has turned the middlemen, like Bushing's Minnesota gofer, into dealers in their own right. Folks like Eaton, and Bushing in his early days, who advertised their goods in small-print ads in sports memorabilia magazines, had to make eBay part of their supply chain. Now they scour it for bargains and sell them—often after fixing the gloves up—for a profit of $20 or $50 or maybe $200 if they get lucky. The best eBay hunters look for misspellings or vague descriptions to find gloves no one else knows exist on the site.

Prices have also been affected by eBay. It made it apparent just how ubiquitous some gloves are—like Mickey Mantle kids' models or Wilson's Harvey Kuenn gloves. "I was selling [Mantles] for $400 to $500, and I knew, these guys are going to realize someday there are about 80 million Mickey Mantle gloves out there," Bushing says. Still, a common glove generally gets a better price on eBay than from a magazine ad, because

An eBay listing for a rare Joe DiMaggio Spalding 222-189 claimed it was as "soft as Marilyn's skin."

only savants read the ads; on eBay you pull in the casual collectors, dads looking for gifts and nostalgic fans looking for an item to put over the fireplace. If they liked Harvey Kuenn, they'll start a bidding war and pay $80 for a $30 Wilson 2120 with his signature stamped inside.

But eBay fails the high-ticket seller. Top gloves rarely fetch their full value because rich collectors don't bother to shop on eBay. They haunt auctions mounted by MastroNet, Leland's, or Hunt, and they pay what they must to secure something that takes their collections up a notch. "In every multimillion dollar memorabilia collection, there are a few top-shelf game-worn gloves," says Bushing. Despite its super-computers, eBay can't say what its most expensive glove fetched. Some collectors remember a $6,000 Lou Gehrig–endorsed fielder's glove a few years ago—a far cry from the $387,500 Gehrig gem.

With all the activity, however, eBay and other auction sites can be seedy places. Despite threats displayed on the site, sellers routinely "warm up" auctions, acting as serious bidders to raise the price for their own items. There's a more nefarious kind of fraud, too. Last year, a Babe Ruth model turned out to be worth far less than its eBay sales price, as the silver lettering rubbed off suspiciously when the buyer wiped the glove. A suit in small-claims court ensued. In a case of an innocent mistake, a twenties handball glove was sold as an 1890s finger-less baseball glove. The attraction was the "tornado palm," circular stitching that simply didn't appear in 1890s baseball gloves. Needless to say, the handball glove wasn't worth a tiny fraction of the $1,500 final price. (It's not just eBay collectors who make mistakes, though. Recently the Baseball Hall of Fame graciously removed a similar twenties handball glove when Phillips, Bushing, and others proved it was not a 19th-century baseball glove.)

And it's easy to come away from an Internet glove auction downright disappointed. You can't see mildew in a picture, and a mildewed glove is like a dirty dog. So smart bidders pepper the seller with e-mails asking about a glove's smell—and lots of other things as well: the suppleness of the leather, the strength of the stitching, the presence of "chafing" or "checking" (worn or cracked leather) inside. They ask for the glove's size, as often the pictures offer no frame of reference. Some collectors ask where the glove has lived, swearing old gloves from the South, where the summers are hotter and the winters still humid, are dicier propositions than Yank gloves. But maybe those folks just have too much time on their hands.

Still, the hobby turns out more than its share of novelties. There are gloves of charming provenance: Seth Swirsky, a Beverly Hills collector, has the glove Dizzy Dean wore in 1947 when he came out of the broadcast booth, and out of retirement, to pitch four innings of shutout ball for the St. Louis Browns after complaining on the air about the team's pitchers. The glove is a Goldsmith Pete Reiser JCL model. And there are coincidences, as when the first two known gloves with the endorsement of WWI-era first baseman Jack Fournier showed up hundreds of miles apart within two weeks of each other a few years ago. Or when a collector found a glove with "BEN CRENSHAW" inked on it in a Longview, Texas, baseball card shop, purchased originally at the golfer's mother's garage sale.

Autograph shows are always eventful: Carlton Fisk and Dave Concepción have each refused to sign a gamer, claiming the gloves had been stolen from them years before. And Johnny Bench and Joe Pepitone both have fallen back in love with a former glove when asked to sign it at a card show.

Both asked to buy the glove back and both were turned down.

And there's beginner's luck. Several years ago Greg Rubano, a Rhode Island collector, found a thirties Babe Ruth Spalding for $3. "Your glove-finding days don't get any better from here on," Phillips told him. The glove is worth at least $500 now.

But are there such finds today? At the dawn of the glove-collecting era, Ryan Petty self-published *What Smart Dealers Know About Baseball Gloves*. It's full of wisdom, except maybe for this: "The baseball glove craze will be obvious by 1993 and will last until 1995, and then the market will plateau." Experts say they still haven't seen a plateau in the availability of lower-priced gloves. Those gloves are turning up anew at flea markets and being recycled on eBay; they feed the fan's desire to feel special and worthy. Expensive gloves are rare by definition. Only six 19th-century fingerless gloves are known to exist today. But more will turn up, in attics or garages. Find one and you're at least $15,000 richer. Now *that* should stir those competitive juices.

Index